zen

and the art of

gardening

zen

and the art of

gardening

gill hale

SOURCEBOOKS, INC.®
NAPERVILLE, ILLINOIS

contents

the zen approach

to gardening

These days, bombarded by stimuli in our homes, at work, and at play, it is difficult to make sense of our lives and to determine what is important. The closer we get to nature and to our roots, the easier it becomes to grasp what is real, and what illusion.

Many have written about the part played by the garden in helping them to connect with what is important in life, and to understand its meaning. The garden has always featured in the lives and activities of those seeking enlightenment through Zen.

When a garden

is used as a place for thought,

that is when a Zen garden

comes to life.

When you

contemplate a garden like this,

it will form a lasting impression

on your heart.

Muso Soseki

taking the first steps

The aim of Zen is to reveal *dharma*, the true natural law. Having reached a point where it is possible to see beyond immediate and unnecessary suffering caused by perceived needs and desires, Zen students will free themselves from the endless cycle of birth and death, and come to understand that what is real is consciousness. Discarding all feelings and pre-formed thought from the mind, students learn to employ themselves instead in meditation.

along the Zen path

Teachers offer their students *koans*, questions to be meditated upon until enlightenment is reached. Only once they have perceived the essence of the questions could they move on to the next. In this way, students follow their master's teachings, while bearing responsibility for the amount of work they put in. There is very little dogma in Zen, merely prescriptions for practice and experience.

Zen and the art

This book will not make you Zen nor help you to understand it. This is only possible through your own experiences. My life has led me into the worlds of information and education, and I have been touched by Western medicine, psychology, and religion. Environmental design, my own and other people's, is my latest preoccupation, in particular the concepts offered to us by ancient philosophies from the East. For me, there has been one constant—a need to connect with the natural world—I have achieved this through gardening. There is little room in our busy, technology-driven lives to connect with the natural world, or wonder at the universe of which we are a part.

# of gardening

Only in the garden can I divorce myself from the relentless bombardment of stimuli, problems, decisions, and responsibilities which make up life in the twenty-first century. By immersing myself in building a compost heap, sowing seeds, and even washing pots, I can be at peace. By sitting still in the garden I become aware of the myriad inter-actions between people and wildlife, plants and the cosmos which go to make up the garden. By growing my own food, I can celebrate the great universal cycle with the same emotions as our ancestors, from sowing to growth, from disintegration to regeneration.

a beginner's mind

A beginner's mind is receptive and to be so it has to be empty. This fundamental concept is a great hurdle for those beginning their Zen journey.

An empty mind has neither cravings to be filled, nor any attachment to knowledge or prejudice. It is therefore free to accept every new experience in a unique way, as if seeing it for the first time, connecting with it, wondering at it, and then detaching from it. The concept of emptiness is very different in the East and the West. In the West, if we place a pot in the garden or a vase on a table, the expectation is that we should fill it with something. In the East, an empty vessel is perceived very differently, as something alive with possibilities. A circle in the East is regarded as a symbol of the universe and the continuous line to eternity. In the West, it is seen as an enclosed space, a hole, something round and complete. The beginner's mind is like the East's perception of a circle, open, compassionate, always fresh and ready to receive each new experience with new eyes.

Everything in the universe has form—our bodies, plants, trees. Nothing exists in isolation from anything else, and nothing is static. Take a seed. We may perceive it as a small hard shell, but when planted, it will soon transform into a plant, ever changing as it grows, matures, and regenerates itself in the form of other seeds. Even an inanimate object like a wheelbarrel, does not remain the same forever. Buddhism allows for change and impermanence.

Change and development are part of this natural order, and we would stagnate if they were not. We have the ability within us to change and grow, but not always the wisdom to channel it in the right way. Zen offers us a way of achieving that wisdom. Since so much of what happens to us is beyond our control, and it is not possible to predict the future any more than we can undo the past, by constantly focussing on them we miss what is happening now. Will our seed order arrive on time, will it be sunny on Thursday, or will the aphids attack the beans? The answer is to have no expectation. We have no control over these circumstances, we have to work with what is and go with the flow.

a still mind

One day I stood in the garden staring at a difficult patch of ground, wondering what to plant there. As it often happens when I do this, my thoughts started wandering—the events of the day, dinner, the possibilities of this plant or that tree, the best nursery to buy the plant, the length of time it would take, coffee, my father's birthday present, and so on. After a while, I was just standing, watching the scenarios in front of me; the blackbird seeing off the robin, the robin diving beak first into the soil to retrieve insects, the bees on the beans. A knock behind me brought me out of my trance and I turned to see the family, noses squashed against the window, watching. Apparently, I had been standing there for over an hour. An hour well spent, not time wasted, an hour in which my mind had stilled and I had become at one with my environment. A still mind brings clarity of thought, removes the excess baggage which forms part of our everyday thought process. A clear mind brings with it the ability to undertake our daily tasks more easily. Dinner was a success that evening, since I was able to concentrate on it without the myriad of other unrelated thoughts that usually accompany the process. Any detachment from the rest of the world and the cares of the day will leave you more prepared to deal with life's tasks efficiently and effectively and will bring you nearer to realization.

the eight

The eight paramitas help us concentrate on what is important, in life and in every activity.

They are not designed as a straight jacket to classify and restrict our activities, but rather as a guide to the process of what we do. Each chapter in this book represents a meditation, each in turn expands upon an individual principle to help us employ Zen principles in the garden.

meditations

To live by Zen principles is to achieve enlightenment, and those who achieve enlightenment, achieve Buddahood. "Zen," suggests Sangharakshita, "is merely a voice crying—wake up, wake up." I am at the beginning of my journey.

I invite you to share it with me as we explore *Zen and the Art of Gardening*.

chapter 1

right thought: planning

Meditation: "We are what we think. All that we are

arises with our thoughts. With our thoughts we make the world." Buddha

When we have a beginner's mind we are receptive to what each day brings. We approach it with courage and with an open mind and heart. Thoughts can color the image we have of ourselves and of those around us and the places where we live. Negative thoughts are a deterrent to living and experiencing life to the fullest and are usually the result of bad experiences in the past, or fear for the future. "The worst fear," said Theodore Roosevelt, "is the fear of living." Living a Zen lifestyle suggests no attachment to the past or to the future, leaving the way open to living and experiencing every moment in the here and now.

Zen suggests that we should live in the moment. There is, however, a subtle difference between the expectation that things will just fall into place, and having a good design, which will allow for evolution and change and for each component to work in harmony with the others. By merely analyzing something and breaking it down into its constituent parts—as is often a Western approach—we lose sight of the whole picture. People in the East approach everything they do—be it gardening, painting, calligraphy, or cooking—with the same focus and understanding of the fundamental natures of the ingredients they are using and of the way these work together. Indeed, in considering a Zen approach to garden design, it is important to look beyond what we find available in the local garden center, to the fundamental concepts behind gardening. The concepts are universal; it is our understanding of their meaning and expression of them which makes them Zen.

knowledge

"Knowledge is to be acquired only by corresponding experience. How can we know what we are told merely?"

In the fifteenth century text "Illustrations for Designing Mountain, Water, and Hillside Field Landscapes" Zoen, a priest, suggested that, "If you have not received the oral transmission, you must not make gardens." This indicates why in the East it takes so long for garden designers to be considered experienced enough to create gardens. Students are apprenticed to a master in all the arts and practice only when their master considers them ready. While their forefathers were using their esoteric knowledge in gardening to harness the energies of the earth and the universe for the power and advancement of their rulers and emperors, peasant farmers were harnessing them for their livelihoods. They used an intuitive understanding of their locality to select sheltered sites and observation of the movement of the sun and moon and subtle changes on the land to select good planting times. Much of this information was passed down the generations orally. However, it is only through experience that it becomes possible to attain the necessary skills, and attune the senses to the environment. With this type of empowerment, we can employ the Zen arts in the garden to understand the dynamic and nurturing qualities of gardening.

imperfect

practice

Many years ago I set out to do some woodwork. Nothing too ambitious, just a small cold frame. The instruction manual informed me about equipment and method, but what it could not help me with was the practice. My sawing left the edges of the lid wavy. Undaunted, I tried my hand with the chisel, which slipped almost instantly. The local hospital reunited half of my finger with the other half. A week later, I returned to tackle the strange angles on the side of the lid. Sandpaper was unequal to the task, and I turned again to the chisel, and once again sliced one finger in two. The nurse was polite, but suggested that some people take much longer than others to learn from experience. With me in the casualty department was a mother with two young children. The third had just been admitted for stomach pumping, having eaten laburnum seeds. Both his siblings had been pumped before him for the same reason. I have not touched a chisel since, except to use it as a screwdriver (which broke it anyway), sensing that my talents lay elsewhere. I wonder what was the fate of the laburnum tree?

the journey

People often ask me

"Is the garden finished—are you there yet?"

To me, the whole thing
about the garden is the journey,
getting to the point,
rather than actually being
at that point—
enjoying things on the way.

Will Giles Garden Designer

The more we journey in life, the clearer it becomes that most of what we accumulate around us, including the thoughts, hopes, and fears that we experience, are meaningless. We can plan our journey meticulously, but the unexpected will often happen to throw us off course. Change is part of life. Even if we hoe the same row of beans twice, the experience will never be the same. For example, the beans will have grown from week to week, the aphids may have arrived, and the robin may not be sitting on the pole this time.

Fear of change is brought about by dependency; letting go of self-doubt, fear, prejudice, and attachment opens up infinite possibilities for new experiences and enables us to be receptive. The universe will provide—if we allow it to.

"Find a little piece of land somewhere and plant a carrot seed. Now sit down and watch it grow. When it is fully grown, pull it up, and eat it."

Alice Bay Laurel

approach

In order to create a Zen garden, we have to be involved in the process. However wonderful our gardens are and however much we enjoy them, if they are designed and managed by others, or if we treat them as merely an extension of our living space, they are not necessarily in the spirit of a Zen garden. The popularity of garden make-over programs and the resultant increase in activity at garden stores suggests that people are becoming increasingly aware of the necessity for a more natural lifestyle, or are lured by the idea of an outdoor room. Through a process of discovery and experience, many people achieve gardens that could be considered Zen—from the smallest window box or balcony to vast expanses.

the window box

My grandmother was a country girl who, following the disruption of the First World War and her subsequent marriage and widowhood, found herself living in a tiny tenement flat in London. Along with two hundred others, her windows overlooked a large concrete play area. There was no mistaking which windows were hers. Throughout the year, her window boxes shone out like beacons. Her father had been a gardener and it was obviously in her blood—the yearning for the open-air existence of her youth. Daffodils glowed in early spring, followed by pansies, and then *antirrhinums* until the first frosts, when the boxes, replanted with daffodil bulbs, would go under my grandmother's bed until they sprouted. The windows behind the boxes shone due to a weekly ritual, which saw her suspended, bottom out, three floors up, polishing so she could appreciate the flowers properly. In tending her window boxes, my grandmother was recreating the open meadows and cottage gardens of her youth, in much the same way as Buddhist monks reduce the mountains and river valleys of Japan to rock and raked gravel in their temple gardens.

Old Meg she was a Gipsy
And liv'd upon the Moors:
Her bed it was the brown heath turf,
And her home was out of doors.

Her apples were swart blackberries,
Her currants, pods o'broom;
Her wine was dew of the wild white rose,
Her book a churchyard tomb.

Her Brothers were the craggy hills,
Her Sisters larchen trees—
Alone with her great family
She liv'd as she did please.

No breakfast had she many a morn,
No dinner many a noon,
And 'stead of supper she would stare,
Full hard against the Moon.

merrilies

But every morn, of woodbine fresh
She made her garlanding,
And, every night, the dark glen Yew
She wove, and she would sing.

And with her fingers old and brown
She plaited Mats o' Rushes,
And gave them to the Cottagers
She met among the Bushes.

Old Meg was brave as Margaret Queen
And tall as Amazon:
An old red blanket cloak she wore;
A chip-hat had she on.
God rest her aged bones somewhere—
She died full long agone!

John Keats

a
zen
life

When I was about nine years old, I went for a drive with my grandmother and ended up in the country town where she was born. As we sat down on a bench in the marketplace, she pointed to an old lady on another bench—eccentric to say the least, in trousers, most unusual for ladies of her age at the time, and a Trilby hat. "That's my sister." We went over. Part of my early educational experience was having to learn a poem a week; this involved spluttering through it while standing on a wooden bench in total humiliation. I was struggling that particular weekend with "Meg Merrilies" by John Keats—and here she was before me. I can still remember being mesmerized by her skin—glowing brown with huge, tough looking wrinkles. They had not seen each other or made contact for fifty years. After ten minutes catching up with the news, conversation dried up and her sister left. There were no "if onlys," nor did either of them suggest keeping in touch. Like ships in the night, they had passed. A truly Zen experience. She had never married and remained in the cottage of their birth until the area had been developed twenty years before. She had taken to living in a caravan in the field she loved, as free as a bird, with no attachments. We heard many years later that she had died in her sleep, in her mid seventies.

design for the garden

There are universally accepted components to good design. The Zen way of garden design is to develop an intuitive sense of design by observation of the natural world in which we live. This is not to say that we cannot put our individual stamp on our garden, but just that there are some fundamental considerations to be taken into account.

When we copy a style from a culture other than our own, we sometimes get hooked into the images used.

In the East, animals are used to describe directions. Taken at face value, our gardens could end up with a stone image of a black tortoise placed in the north, but the word "tortoise" in the East conjures up the image of protection, certain weather conditions, air quality, and specific constellations among a myriad of other associations. True, the positioning of a tortoise in the north would represent all these associations to the Eastern mind, but in Western gardens, it is just another ornament.

In Japan, courtyard gardens, like those in the temples, often contain elements which represent the wider landscape. Standing stones can represent Mount Fuji and gravel or moss can represent the surrounding seas and landscapes. A single plant

position

"You take strong seeds and plant them in a good spot in the sun, most will grow quickly, but some seeds can't live with very strong sun. You have to follow natural forces; the seasons, the climate, even day and night, and respect the basic nature of the seed."

Takashi Yoshikawa

can represent the forests. Japanese people, wherever they live in the world, can capture the spirit of their own land using such imagery. To a Texan living on the edge of a desert, such imagery would be meaningless, as would a cacti garden to a Scot.

To follow the Zen route is to create a garden which fits into the surroundings in which it has been planted. Where we live will impact on what we can achieve in the garden. Conditions by the coast are very different to a secluded garden in a valley in the middle of the countryside. We can fight against nature and attempt to create a seaside garden in the middle of a wood, or a lush shady garden on top of a mountain, but achieving this would be a struggle. We would be fighting a losing battle against the natural characteristics of the land.

In the East, geomancers determine auspicious positions for houses, dependent on the type of energy coming from each direction. Ourselves and our plants need protection from the wind and access to sun and water to thrive. Equally, we may be vulnerable to intrusion and from being overlooked by unsightly structures, and we will need to address this in the garden.

right plant,
right place

Plant positions are important and they each have requirements with regard to light, shade, soil conditions, and aspect. Whether they face east or south can make the difference between them thriving or just muddling through. We like to live in comfortable surroundings; the same principle applies with plants and their placement in the garden. If ever there were a reason for not following a fixed formula in design, plant positions would be it.

Feng shui, the ancient art of placement, is extremely popular with gardeners as it encourages them to place things in certain directions to pick up the energy of the particular direction and its corresponding element. We are often encouraged to place red plants in the south, which is logical since red plants—like pelargoniums and salvias—thrive in sun and in hot countries, in southern aspects.

However, these formulas were drawn up in ancient China, where the ideal location for building a house was with its back to the north, facing south with a wide open vista to the front. Red flowers planted on the southern plain at the front would therefore thrive. However, in the West we do not all have these conditions. Even where we have a south-facing garden, we will probably have a fence on our southern boundary. Any plants planted against it would therefore be in its shade and facing north, governed by northern conditions. When practiced with understanding, feng shui is an amazing design tool. When there is no understanding, it can create difficulties.

time

In spring, hundreds of flowers;
in autumn, the harvest moon;
In summer, a refreshing breeze;
In winter, snow will be there with you.
If useless thoughts do not lurk in your mind
Any season is a good season for you.

thirteenth century Chinese koan

Timing is important. In choosing the most appropriate time of the year to undertake various activities like pruning and building, we will be going with the flow of nature. By adopting the Zen approach to gardening, we become aware of nature's patterns and work with them. Pruning at the wrong time may affect the plants' growth next season.

Everything is subject to biorhythms, the daily and annual cycles of the sun and the moon which affect the patterns of behavior in every living thing. Our ancestors were conscious of the migratory habits of certain insects and birds and the growth cycles of plants, and used the moon and stars as indicators for the best times to sow their crops.

The seasons are determined by the passage of the sun. While in some parts of the world the seasonal boundaries are not very distinct, in Europe and much of the East there are four seasons, still marked by festivals suggesting the start of spring and the beginning of growth to the final harvest thanksgiving and the winter rest period.

Where we plant to recognize the seasons, we will ensure a plentiful supply of food throughout the year as well as offering ourselves something to marvel at each day.

the view

Since the great landscape gardens of the eighteenth century, the "borrowed view" has been part of the vocabulary of garden designers in the West. The industrial middle classes created their sweeping gardens to take in views of the landscapes beyond their boundaries, and planted clumps of trees, channeling views to statues and temples inspired by ancient Greece and Rome. In the East, the term *shakkei* does not suggest merely borrowing a distant view, but literally capturing it alive by incorporating it into the design of the garden itself, so that it is not obvious where one stops and the other begins.

It is perfectly possible to capture the tiniest scene within a garden by judicious planting. The Yuan-yeh suggests four methods: "borrowing from a great distance, borrowing from nearby, borrowing from a high level, and borrowing from a low level." Planted carefully, trees and shrubs can frame notable views, plants, and other features to draw them into a design. They can also be used to draw the eye away from a feature which is unsightly. A tree placed right in front of an unsightly building often draws attention to it. Planted slightly to the side, with the branches softening the edge and balanced by another further away, the eye can be drawn away. Telephone poles are a necessary modern eyesore, but it is perfectly possible not to see them if we plant to distract rather than try to camouflage them.

privacy

Gardens are often enclosed to create privacy. In the West, the aim is to exclude the outside world totally. In the East, openings are always left in walls and fences, connecting those living within to the outside world. Known as "moon gates," these openings are often intricately carved latticework, but it is possible to create openings in hedges simply through careful pruning. Windows are positioned to draw the garden into the house and many houses are designed with a central garden courtyard to make the garden accessible from every room. Connection with the world outside and with the universe is a fundamental part of Eastern philosophy, and every art form incorporates symbols of the trinity of the heavens, the earth, and human beings.

illusions of grandeur

I recently saw a photograph of a delightful garden where the planting within the garden was contoured to offer a view through to the rolling hills and woodland beyond, the effect being the continuation of the garden for as far as the eyes could see. Unfortunately, a wooden bridge had been placed across the foreground planting, creating a barrier within the garden and spoiling the illusion. Sometimes this happens in gardens, in which mirrors have been placed to make the garden look bigger. A mirror is an effective ploy to create an illusion of space in a small garden. However, avoid creating a visual stop (for example, by placing a pot in front of the mirror) which draws attention to the mirror rather than allowing the eye to wander through, seemingly into another garden.

the elements

There is a system in the East which classifies everything in the universe into five elements—wood, fire, earth, metal, and water—which determines the particular qualities associated with such considerations as color and shape. The elements work with each other in perceived patterns and so it is possible to tell at a glance which colors will blend or clash, and which combination of shapes will work well together. They also relate to the sense organs (eyes, ears, nose, tongue, and skin) and to the sense objects (form, sound, smell, taste, and touch). By themselves, each element is empty. It is the mind which brings all the elements together and enables us to see the whole picture and pick out imbalances where they occur. The system evolved thousands of years ago, drawn from observation of the natural world.

If we take the elements at face value, the garden will be lacking a life force. Where we employ the mind and work with nature, we can draw on them to create a Zen space.

the plants

Horticulturists constantly strive to create bigger and better plants—to improve on nature. In *The Garden Plants of China*, Peter Valder suggests that Western visitors to Chinese gardens are often disappointed at the comparatively few plants grown there, particularly since over 30,000 Chinese plants have found their way into Western gardens. In the East, plants are chosen for their growth patterns and beauty and also for their symbolism in the culture of each country. In the West, the trend is to plant in groups. Clumps of trees or plants which blend together to form a mass is the preferred style. In the East, the emphasis is more on the individual plants, and the more gnarled the tree or the more distinct the shape, the more evocative the image to the Eastern mind.

flow

There are some places that feel alive and vibrant, and others to which we are indifferent or which have a depressing effect on us.

Whatever the reason—the lie of the land, the quality of the air, the fertility of the soil—gardens which make us feel good are imbued with what is known in the East as chi, or *prana* in India. In the West, we have no similar concept, but it can be expressed as the life force or spirit of a place. By working with nature and the natural forces in our gardens, we can create an environment which feels alive.

When we walk in the countryside, we always stumble across something which interests us—a magnificent tree, a rare flower, a clearing in the woods, a distant view. We can create such areas in the garden, which we approach with anticipation and which reward our progress. Occasionally, when visiting a garden, I start down a path with great anticipation, only to reach a dead end. To have to turn back is disappointing, whereas a gate in the wall would have rewarded my efforts and encouraged me on, or a seat would have encouraged me to stay awhile and be still. The pathways we create are like a journey—too straight and we will rush down them and notice nothing on the way; gently curved, and we will walk slowly, and observe.

yin
yang

The way a garden feels has to do with the placement of its components in relation to each other. A garden does not feel balanced if there is too much of any one thing—types of plants, shapes of leaves, hard landscaping, color, or anything else.

In the East, the concept of yin and yang governs much of garden design. It is the theory of the balance of complementary opposites. If we have a concept of what "up" signifies, then by the nature of things, there must be a concept of "down" or "up" would be meaningless. If we pave over the whole of the backyard, then there will be no balance, but a paved area complemented by plants will work. The New Northern approach to design, led by designers in mainland Europe, uses drifts of natural looking planting. This can paint tapestries on the landscape and look magical, but when one type of plant is used, the result is unbalanced. The latest trend is for using grasses and sedges. In the natural world, they would be interspersed with other kinds of plants and those with broad leaves to complement and balance the effect. Planted all together in large beds, the effect is lifeless and the beds look unkempt and uninteresting for much of the year.

To be
conscious
that you are ignorant,
is the
greatest step
to
knowledge

Benjamin Disraeli

attitude

There is no doubt that the deeper you search into any subject, the more you realize just how much more there is to learn. However, we do not have to know everything and we do not need to impress others with our knowledge. In the Zen garden, we work steadily and quietly. "Still waters run deep," suggests a wise person, but still it is not quite the Zen way.

To journey the Zen way is to be unattached and light headed—like a child. Humility is a virtue which is useful to cultivate. How can we fail to feel humble in the garden when most of what occurs there is beyond our comprehension? Others can guide us, but it is the natural world that holds the key to understanding.

Lengthy apprenticeships in the East now seem strange to us and we often think we can learn all we need to know from books or by searching the Internet. Like teachers, books and articles can act only as guides. We have to work and experience for ourselves before we really understand how things work. The Zen way is to let go of the need to accumulate everything we can about a subject and to take things slowly and calmly.

the inspiration– visiting gardens

One of the greatest privileges I know is to be able to snoop around other people's gardens. Zen gardeners take a lot of their inspiration from the natural world and by visiting other gardens we can learn so much about what works and which plants look well together, as well as drawing on the vast range of knowledge that other people have. This is not to say that we should copy blindly what we see, but we can borrow ideas and reinterpret them within our own gardens.

growing

The Green Thumb program in New York is known worldwide thanks to intervention of actress Bette Midler when the City Council was all set to bulldoze the tranquil spaces which were created, over many years, on derelict land on street corners. During a recent trip, a New Yorker led me into areas where tourists rarely venture. Divided into small sections, each garden is developed by local individuals who plant flowers and vegetables, make artwork out of anything they can lay hands on, and use the space as a meeting place or somewhere to just sit and watch the world go by. Each plot is inspirational and a work of art, yet hanging over them all is the constant threat of being bulldozed. Some have been saved, but with land at a premium, a developer's money speaks louder than a plea for an oasis. Maria Soares has been working her plot in the 6A and Avenue B Garden in the Lower East Side for thirty years, in one of the few gardens officially exempt from extinction. When I asked her why the garden was so important to her, Maria said she felt that she was working for God; by working the land and creating a special place which others could enjoy after her, she felt that she was doing His work here on earth.

the big apple

"I like going to the garden early on Sunday mornings. I slap on my headphones, listen to Mozart, and putter. After a while, I take a breather and sit in the gazebo, just watching the flowers grow.

One Sunday, there I was with muddy knees and bits of weeds in my hair when a very proper lady wearing little white gloves passed by. I must have startled her when she spotted me. Quite loudly, she commented about my sitting around and not going to church.

I didn't say a word. How could I explain I was already there?"

Johanna Sherman, The Bayview Gardens, Coney Island, Brooklyn

chapter 2

right action: considering

"We didn't inherit

the land from our fathers. We are borrowing it for our children." Amish saying

Living a Zen life style suggests that we take responsibility for our actions, and inherent in this is that we are aware of the consequences of what we do to other people and to the earth.

We are part of an ecological system made up of many parts. Between us and the lowly amoeba, there are billions of microorganisms involved in the food chain which keeps us alive. Each insect, bird, and animal plays a part in the ecosystem of its environment and each plant and tree provides food or shelter.

Since each link in the chain is important to our own well-being, it is to our advantage to live in harmony with our neighbours in the natural world. In Zen, the ultimate goal is enlightenment and in the garden we are usually working towards the completion of a task or a design, and to reach a greater understanding in techniques and growing patterns.

With every action we take comes responsibility. The way in which we achieve it is the ultimate goal.

"Let everything be allowed to

grand
gestures

A significant gesture we can make to our successors is to leave them the world as we found it, so that they too can experience the diversity of plant and animal species and can inherit a world which will support and keep them and their descendants. We are becoming aware of the devastating effects our uninformed actions can have on the natural world and there is a growing concern for the environment. A Zen approach ensures that we act in an informed and ethical way.

do what it naturally does, so that its nature will be satisfied." Chuang Tzu

family tree

I recently met a lady who lives in Kent, in the south of England, who decided to plant a forest. She did not just purchase her favorite trees, but researched which trees were indigenous to the area and how they grow naturally in the wild. She approached the Forestry Commission, who helped her with a plan of how to mix the trees and in which proportions and how far apart to plant them. She then planted every tree herself and has the pleasure of knowing them individually and watching their progress as they grow to maturity in her lifetime, knowing that they will outlive her children and probably their grandchildren, and they will seed themselves to ensure that their heritage will be continued for generations to come.

felling

"The true gardener must be brutal and imaginative for the future."
Vita Sackville-West

trees

I meet people from time to time who think it is an offense to remove a tree. It is often impossible not to move it, because it is diseased, because it has outgrown its space, or is in danger of undermining the foundations of the house or damaging the drains. Few of us would chop down a mature tree without giving it a lot of thought, but the fact of the matter is, some trees are in the wrong place, or perhaps, more accurately, we build houses in the wrong place. We plant trees that we have often purchased on a whim at the garden center when they are quite small. They can simply outgrow their space. This is why it is so important to know your plants, their needs and habits, and their ultimate heights and girths. Sometimes we want to remove a tree simply because we want to create an entirely new garden and it does not play a part in the plan. If it salves your conscience, explain the situation to it, thank it for being part of the garden for such a long time, make a seat out of it, and leave chunks of it around to provide shelter for wildlife, and replace it with something more appropriate.

making

When we make do, we will not feel the same way about what we have acquired as we would if we had selected it because it was special. The plants I dislike most in my garden are those which others have given me, and I have had to plant for fear of giving offense, and those purchased in the company of someone else who assures you that the pile of twigs you see before you in the pot will turn into something you will love. I find myself never quite giving unsolicited donations the care and attention I give those I have selected myself for a specific place or purpose, or those which have arrived by magic because they want to be there. Similarly, I find myself severely hacking back plants I have purchased under pressure; this of course makes them grow even more vigorously, in direct opposition to my subconscious intention to make them go away. For plants that seem to overwhelm an area of the garden and have to be constantly cut back, a better solution would be to place them where they have a free reign to follow their natures. The Zen way is to love, and when you give love, those you give it to will thrive and return it.

do

long-term planning

We sometimes choose plants to solve an immediate problem and because of this, they have, within a year or two, become an even greater one. The "Mile a Minute Vine," *Polygonum baldschuanicum* and Clematis montana are delightful plants in the right place, but when grown to create some privacy, you create problems for both parties since they grow so fast and need regular lopping to keep them under control. Far better to choose something which grows more slowly and will fill the space eventually with little maintenance, which both you and your neighbor will appreciate.

soil

We can do no better for our plants than to create a fertile healthy soil. Soil consists of decayed vegetation—twigs, leaves, flowers, manure, the bones of animals and birds, and the husk-like shells of scaled insects. Add to that ground-up rock, mineral and trace elements, and over a million microorganisms and miles of fungal filaments per cupful of soil and the result is not dirt, but a living breathing organism. Each microorganism has its own unique part to play. Some act as decomposers, breaking down decaying plant material. Others make the resulting nutrients, released into the soil, available to plant roots. Some deal with unwelcome nematodes which could damage plants, and others attach themselves to plant roots to improve a plant's supply of certain minerals and trace elements, or release them into the soil for the benefit of surrounding plants.

in praise of worms

In healthy soil, there are likely to be over one hundred earthworms per square yard. In a year, they will ingest enough soil to produce eight pounds of nutrient-rich fertilizer in the form of castings. Worm casts are five times higher in minerals than the surrounding soil, and are therefore to be treasured. While vegetable growers are only too pleased to invite earthworms onto their plot, those in love with their lawns are not best pleased at the coiled casts they find there. Rather than go the elimination route, we can make good use of the casts and sweep them into the grass to feed it instead of using high cost chemical fertilizers. If we collect the casts they provide us with a soil tonic or for use in potting compost or a top dressing for pot plants. Earthworms weave through the soil helping to aerate it and channel water in, thus improving conditions for their coworkers. In time, earthworm action can help change excessively acid or alkaline soils to a more neutral pH to accommodate a wider range of plants.

In woodland, fallen
leaves, spent plant material, and
wildlife which have reached the end of
their cycle, rot down in situ to provide a fertile
medium for the trees and the plants which will
grow there next year, as well as providing
protection for over-wintering flora and fauna.

in praise of compost

Compost in the garden improves the soil, not only by fertilizing it, but also because its bulk acts as a water-retaining agent. Following the lead of the natural world, the best place to use compost is in the place which generated it. I have occasionally used compost made from material from the shrub and perennial part of the garden in the area in which I grow vegetables. It is noticeable that the vegetables do not do as well as those in compost made primarily from material from the vegetable garden. Again, we have to take the needs of each individual plant into consideration. Some plants—such as lavender, buddleia, and ceanothus—prefer to be left to their own devices and do not like a fertile soil.

the art of

Ingredients

Anything which has once been alive
can go on to the compost heap.
Plant material
Vegetable kitchen waste
Dust from the vacuum bag
Hair
Spent hops
Brown cardboard
Unbleached and unprinted paper
Bird and rodent corpses
Grass mowings
Seaweed
Compost from an old heap to
introduce microorganisms

leave out

Corpses of large animals
Anything cooked
Anything synthetic
Meat
Wood from Evergreens
Trees
Dog and cat manure
Privet
Poisonous plants
Diseased plant material
Chemicals

compost making

mix with

Nettles

Diluted nettle juice

Blood and bone/hoof and horn/fish meal
    (sprinkle a handful every foot or so)

A little water if the ingredients are dry

Air-layer different types of material and mix so the
    heap does not become compressed and airless

compost—methods

Quantities

Use what you have but mix it well first, if possible. If this is not possible and you add the material in layers, it will be useful to turn the heap after a few weeks and replace it in its containers until it is ready.

Always try to mix grass mowings with other materials or they will form a soggy mat.

Separate

- Wood shavings—Sprinkle with soil and liquid manure and add to the main heap the following year.
- Turf—Stack grass side down in heap for a year.
- Twigs thicker than a pencil—Sprinkle with soil and liquid manure and leave until soft, then add to the main heap.
- Leaves—Stack on their own in mesh bins or black plastic sacks. Hose if they get too dry. Leave for a year.

Containers

Containers should stand on the soil to allow the decomposers free access.

Place a layer of twiggy material in the bottom to let in the air. Wooden pallets tied together make excellent containers, and similar versions can be made using wooden slats. Having

and storage

just completed a new kitchen, I had four large, heavy duty cardboard appliance boxes, which worked extremely well for one season. There are a variety of commercially produced plastic bins on the market, with lids and doors which open at the bottom to allow you to fill from the top and collect from the bottom at the same time. I have to admit that I prefer the compost made in these, since it is made quickly and warms up to a temperature high enough to kill off most annual weed seeds. They are also neat, and are suitable for town gardens. The other reason is that I am a wimp. Open heaps need a cover of sorts to keep out excess rain. Anything can be used—sacks, rugs, or more elaborate covers made of corrugated plastic. Whenever I have covered an open heap, I inevitably uncover something furry underneath when I lift it up. Since my compost heaps are in a confined space, the escape route is narrow, and since I cannot find anything remotely cute about a rodent, I prefer the plastic version.

Time

This depends on the time of year, the weather, and the container. A well-made heap can take three months, others up to a year. The compost is ready when it is dark and crumbly and you cannot distinguish the original ingredients. It should smell sweet.

in praise of manure

In traditionally run farms, farmers harvest their crops and then let animals into the fields to graze on the stubble, while at the same time manuring the ground for the following year's crop. In parts of mainland Europe, it is not unusual to see chickens and pigs in orchards, feeding well from fallen fruit and keeping down the pest population, while at the same time providing the trees with valuable fertilizer. The average garden does not lend itself to such practices, but it has to be said that manure is still one of the best ways of keeping a garden well-fed and healthy.

- Manure should never be spread around the garden when it is fresh, as it will scorch the plants.

- Manure should be stacked for a few weeks before it is used on the garden. When manure is fresh and stacked, the heap will get very hot and often steam. When the heap has cooled down, the manure will be ready to use.

- It pays to be picky when selecting manure. Manure from organically reared herbivores is usually fine. Manure from carnivores, including household pests, is best not used. One of the most potent substances is guano, bird droppings, particularly those from seagulls, a limited resource for most of us, though it is available in pelleted form.

gather ye rosebuds

I grew up in West London and lived in apartment with no garden, as did most of my friends. The father of one of them had an allotment. He was a postman, and in those days postmen rode bicycles with large baskets on the front for the letter sack. He had straps on his sack which he carried on his back. His basket was lined with newspaper and had a small shovel in it. At the time, coal was delivered to most homes by horse and cart, beer drawn in barrels by horse and dray, and there were a lot of policemen on horseback because the police stables were close by. We would occasionally see Percy following a horse expectantly on his bike and my friend would always try to distract the attention of whoever she was with by pointing out something of absolutely no interest in a shop window until he had passed. We all knew what he was about though—and his roses were wonderful.

liquid manures

Homeopathic medicine treats people with minuscule doses of a substance in such dilution that it contains scant trace of the substance. Flower essences are also used in microscopic proportions. Farmers and gardeners who follow the teachings of Rudolf Steiner and use Biodynamic methods use the same principle for making liquid manure in homeopathic proportions. Maria Thun, who has researched these methods in Germany for decades, has been largely responsible for bringing them to into the public domain. Cow dung, eggshells, special compost preparations made from plant and mineral extracts, and valerian juice are mixed and left for a few weeks in a bottomless wooden barrel in the ground. Between them, they contain all the nutrients required by a healthy soil, in tiny proportions. At the end of this period, small amounts are diluted in water, stirred and strained, and the resulting spray improves the soil and activates the beneficial soil organisms.

green manures

Green manure is now widely used in gardens to cover the soil in areas waiting to be planted with something else. For soils that are exposed to the elements, the wind can blow it away and too much rain can wash all the nutrients beyond the reach of many plant roots. The roots of green manure crops store up food which can be recycled back into the soil. These crops can be sown at various times of the year and perform different functions:

- Some are legumes and make nitrogen available to other plants, those which grow quickly are inter-cropped with other plants.
- Some live through the winter, keeping the soil open and receptive for spring sowings.

Know the nature of the green manure plants you are using, so that you follow them with a plant from a different family, which can make use of the beneficial substances left by the crop and will not be deprived of any mineral or trace element used up by it. The seed of suitable plants are now widely available through seed merchants.

mulching

Mulching is merely copying what happens naturally—covering the soil with a layer of organic substance to keep the moisture in and protect plant roots to raise the soil temperature, to feed the soil, and to prevent annual weed seed sprouting. Soil, as we have seen, is a living organism. It needs light, moisture, air, and food.

If your garden has been neglected for a number of years and you need to clear it of tougher weeds and brambles, you can keep them down by laying brown cardboard over the soil. Allotment holders are often ridiculed for their use of carpet, but I have found it invaluable when the main growing season ran out on me and I couldn't keep up with the weeds. Hessian backed carpet is the one to use. Foam dries up and turns to powder and makes a mess, and of course it is made with chemicals. Beware also of treated carpets. Newspaper is often recommended as a temporary measure since the ink rarely contains lead these days, but you may not wish to risk it. All these mulches have the advantage that they rot down in a year or two, and help to improve the soil.

Substances to avoid for mulching

Fresh grass mowings

These can be slightly toxic to other plants. It is always recommended, for example, that you do not let grass grow within three feet of the base of a fruit tree. Also, soil microorganisms have to work overtime with fresh materials. In using grass, we can also introduce as many weed seeds as we are trying to eliminate.

Bark and wood chips

We often do not know the origin of the wood and some wood, particularly those of evergreen trees, actually hinders the growth of other plants. Wood chips can introduce diseases when they have not been through the composting process, and it is the practice of some bark suppliers to use chemicals in the production process.

Straw

If you top dress your soil with rotted compost regularly, mulching is not really required, apart from straw under ripening strawberries for a few weeks to keep them clean. Any weeds which make it through the compost are easily pulled out if your soil is good, even those with tap roots. Straw is a favorite mulch, although it may need anchoring with something a bit heavier in the absence of rain, or it may blow away leaving you with green non-edible tubers. The latest potato growing trend is to mulch rather than earth up. This means less work, fewer weeds, and a cleaner crop.

preservation of wildlife

There can be few gardeners who are unaware of the dangers to birds of slug pellets and the dangers to the environment as a whole in the indiscriminate use of chemicals in the garden. Each of us takes personal responsibility for the consequences. We rarely consider the consequences of how we relate to the wildlife we feel privileged to have in the garden, which, like us, have the right to be able to live their lives as nature intended them to. In the wild, animals self regulate. In a well planned garden, even greenfly will not be a problem. If we plant to attract ladybirds and for nesting birds, they will rarely cause damage. It is fashionable to create a nanny state in our gardens for everything that visits, as if they cannot fend for themselves. In doing so, we are in danger of killing by kindness or ignorance.

feeding

Each plant and animal knows instinctively what it needs to survive. How many of us know, for example, that robins need a minute amount of poison, which it finds in crocuses, to get them through the winter?

If we follow the rules of good garden design, we will have a garden which has something to offer all those who participate in it something to feed their needs throughout the year. If we plant perennials and shrubs with berries and leave seed heads on annuals we will provide a plentiful supply of plant food for the birds. A healthy soil full of compost will always provide insects and worms and leaves us plenty too.

I have resident blackbirds. The family has inhabited my *Clematis montana* for the past twenty years. The mother blackbird and I are very close, too close sometimes since she has become so tame. We work as a team. I tickle the ground a bit to expose a few tasty insects and she responds by leaving me a small deposit in thanks.

cooperation

When neighbors put out breadcrumbs, the Zen approach is to accept that the bird has abandoned me for easier pickings next door, but I can't help feeling resentful. What use have they of a blackbird when their whole backyard is concreted over? I worry for the bird. It is a prime target for local cats when it sits in isolation on their garden table. Cats rarely venture into my garden, they know better.

Mutual cooperation.
Give and take.

Blackbirds are responsible for the many empty snail shells we see around the garden—a contribution few of us can afford to be without. So it is surely better to let them choose their own food? When we put out food and water for birds we are making them dependent on us, and encouraging them not to eat all the insects we regard as foe.

with wildlife

A partnership.

Cats are not generally welcomed by gardeners. Research carried out by the Surrey Wildlife Trust, England, in 1995, discovered that each cat living in a town kills between six and nine songbirds a year. In a twelve acre area, this means the loss of over six hundred birds per year, making cats the main reason for the decreasing bird population and the reason we purchase pesticides to do the work the birds would have done for us.

chapter 3

right effort: work

Meditation: "There is not amongst Man

a more laborious life than is that of a good Gard'ner." John Evelyn

There is no doubt that running a garden is a 365 day a year occupation. There is always something to do in the garden. Even in the depths of winter, there are jobs to be undertaken—repairing things, clearing up, and preparing for planting in the following season. Asked what drove him, H.L. Mencken said "I go on working for the same reason that a hen goes on laying eggs." In other words, he has no choice if things are to run smoothly. This may sound as if gardeners would have it any other way. The gardeners I know do it willingly, not seeing it as a chore, but approaching it as a fulfilling and worthwhile occupation which keeps them fit, gets them out of the house and away from the telephone, partner, or children, with the saving grace that it cannot possibly be a selfish act, since everyone benefits from the fruit of their labors.

laborare et orare

Monks have always worked in gardens, not only to feed themselves and to grow herbs for their medicines, but also as a part of their daily ritual of prayer. "Laborare et Orare"—to work is to pray—is a familiar Cistercian saying, written on many a wall as a reminder of the spiritual nature of their toil. The object for monks was to suppress personal emotion, so not for them was the feeling of elation that we allow ourselves from time to time as we spot the first snowdrops, or our favorite peony opens. We are allowed these emotions in the Zen garden, but we must not forget the hard work too, or our joy will be short-lived.

"no work, no food"

There is a Buddhist story about Hyakujo, a Chinese Zen master who, even at the age of eighty used to work with his pupils in the garden, undertaking all the same hard tasks. The students felt sorry that he had to do this, but they realized that if they asked him to stop he would not listen to them. So one day they hid his tools. That evening, Hyakujo refused to eat. He did not eat the next day, nor the next. The students decided that he was angry with them for having hidden his tools, so the next day they returned them. Hyakujo resumed his work and that evening joined them for a meal, with the words "No work, no food."

a stitch in time...

I have observed the weather patterns for the past twenty or so years at peony time. There are those who keep garden diaries and can, at a glance, pick up the influence of weather patterns on plant growth and wildlife behavior. It seems to me—and I have only gut feeling and no specific evidence for this—that the minute peony flowers emerge, it becomes windy and wet, so that each big beautiful flower lasts only a matter of two or three days before being battered to the ground. There are ways to prolong their life, for example, by staking them before they become top heavy; my intention is always there, but I never remember, telling myself after the event that I prefer the natural look.

Staking the peonies initially would take seconds. If I leave it until they are in flower, then however I tie them they always look as though they have just been tied up and not at all natural. Most irritating jobs take only a few minutes or even seconds to put right, but we waste endless energy putting them to the back of our minds where they sit on our conscience; oiling the squeaky wheel on the barrow; plugging the knot hole in the shed before a mouse nests in there; tying up the clematis before it flops over and you lose a leading shoot for a whole season. These can all be dealt with simply and quickly. The Zen way is to be prepared and to direct your effort to what is necessary.

watering

Such a rare occurrence is a British summer, that still, a quarter of a century on, people are discussing the heat wave of 1976. As a commuter, I had limited time to spend in the garden. There was a watering ban that year due to the heat wave, but I rarely water anyway, except of course things in pots, which I keep to a minimum. While my neighbors' beans plants shriveled up, crisped by the sun, mine went from strength to strength. One day I mentioned this to a colleague who also has thriving beans who lived in town during the week and only saw her beans at her country home at the weekend, so did not water either. This got me thinking. When you water straight on to soil with a hose or a can, it is possible to stand in the same spot for twenty minutes and the water will only penetrate the soil to the depth of your thumb nail.

My theory is that in watering ineffectively with cans and hoses, roots remain near the surface, whereas by not watering, they have to dive down much further into the earth and therefore keep cool and do not get baked and die. So my no water policy is still in existence and seems to work well. Anything planted in the ground is on its own after its initial soaking—I always follow the traditional method of "puddling in"—planting in a puddle and then firming in a few minutes later. If it is really hot soon after planting, I'll give new plants a whole can full of water each, but if you plant in the autumn this should not be necessary. Dripper pipes are better than hoses, because the drips drip just where you want them to and do not run off in all directions. Likewise, if you cut the bottom off a plastic bottle and plunge it into the hole with your tomato plants or your squashes, you can channel the water directly to the roots where it needs to be.

watering systems

Greenhouses

Gardeners have to plan meticulously. Unless they take their annual vacation in the winter, they have to ensure that the garden will be able to survive without them. Life is, in many ways, easier now than it has ever been and there are ways to ensure that seedlings and greenhouse plants are kept watered when we are unable to do the task ourselves. Placement on capillary matting fed by a length of fabric with one end in a bucket of water, will be enough for the survival of our treasured plants in our absence. Greenhouse grown seedlings which have germinated but not quite reached the potting on stage by the time we have to leave them for a fortnight, will greet us like triffids when we return, far too spindly to be of use for anything other than compost. Timing is crucial to ensure that they are already in the ground before we go.

Balconies

Those who garden on balconies have never had it easy. The drying winds and the fact that plants have to grow in a limited amount of soil in containers means that watering is a problem. It is now possible to buy gravel in small bags which makes it possible, to some extent, to slow down the evaporation process from the pots, while at the same time keeping the floor of the balcony free from half the contents of each pot as we water. Installing watering systems with timers helps to keep the plants alive and the strategic . placement of spiked drippers distributes the water to just where it is needed in each pot.

washing pots

One of the most hated tasks in the garden is washing pots, particularly around June, when you plant out the half hardy flowers and other things you started in pots. Theoretically I suppose I should wash the pots immediately, but there may be only a few at a time, which hardly seems worth it. As I plant out from April onwards, I stack the pots in sizes in the enormous butler's sink which is my potting bench. By June, when it is full, and the main planting out season is over, I take one size of pot each day and wash them. I choose sunny days on which to do this, so they dry quickly and sit on the back step with a pail of soapy water on my right, one with rinsing water in front and put the washed pots face down on my left. By the time I have finished and emptied the buckets, the pots are dry and I stack them on shelves on either side of the bench, ready for next year. This is a ritual rather than a chore because I only do a certain amount at a time. To do the whole lot in one go would be too much and I would most likely put off doing it. This way works for me, and the gentle, methodical task of washing pots helps to still my mind.

Wu wei is an ancient Chinese precept for living. It means "the path of effortless action," encouraging us to proceed through life "going with the flow," rather than dreaming up complicated, and often expensive, ways of improving the way things are.

to dig, or not to dig?

In those parts of the world which remain comparatively undisturbed by human action, there are no teams of gardeners "double-digging," and incorporating manure and compost into trenches while moving soil from one place to another. It would not be practical and there are several reasons for not doing it. The process is not entirely suitable for the average garden bed today, since it would be impossible to double-dig around shrubs and perennials and we would damage their roots in the process. It is becoming fashionable to mix vegetables with flowers and other plants and not to have separate beds, following the style of the old cottage garden and the French "potager" style. If we look at how things grow naturally, even in the depths of winter, there is never a wide expanse of bare earth. A covering of plants or grass is always there, preventing the wind from blowing the soil away

In China, which has always had a large population to feed, the land is cultivated all year round as one crop immediately follows another, and in Eastern gardens, bare earth rarely shows. Soil bacteria operate in the first few inches or soil and digging drives them further down where they cannot do their job so well. Undug soil remains warmer, enabling the microorganisms to work longer on our behalf and, since the soil is warmer, our plants get off to a good start in the spring. Weed seeds can lay dormant in the soil for years waiting for someone to come along and return them to the top inch or so where they can sprout happily and produce another year's crop. All in all, I cannot see any reason for the backbreaking task of digging, when we can rely on our friends to do it for us without complaint. We still have to dig out the weeds though, don't we? Perhaps we don't. There is another, more natural and less labor intensive method which can help us there too—mulching.

what did I do with the…?

…shears,
string,
scissors,
trowel,
nails,
mallet…

the list is endless.

The garden is the easiest place in the world to get distracted and lose things. We can expend a tremendous amount of wasted effort searching for things we have lost because we did not put them back in their usual place, if indeed they ever had a place.

There are garden tool belts on the market, for shears and pruning knives, but these are impractical for any gardener who bends and kneels a lot. There are various tool-carrying devices, but they are either too shallow, so that things fall out, or they do not have a firm base and topple over. They are usually green and very loseable.

There is an excellent marketing opportunity for someone to devise a reasonably priced, shocking pink plastic basket, with handles, perforated with holes of the right size to let soil but not tools escape, and with a firm enough base to stand upright on slopes. It should be approximately two feet long, one foot high and one foot wide. It would do to carry frequently used small tools around the garden and they could live in it at all times so we can put our hands on anything we need instantly. It would save several hours a month of wasted effort.

garden sheds

Garden sheds are
interesting   places   and
surely a true reflection of the nature of
their owners. Convention and propriety
suggest certain rules and regulations about how the
inside of our homes should appear to the outside world,
but garden sheds are altogether a different story since only
we venture into them—if we can get in. My neighbor at my
first home had his shed at the bottom of the garden, on the
other side of the fence to my compost heap. He spent
many solitary hours there and had created the route to it
like an obstacle course, which he reckoned his wife, a
portly lady and fairly unsteady on her feet, would never
tackle. In it, unbeknown to her, he made wine out of
anything he could think of, and often when I was playing
with my compost heap, a hand would appear over the
fence with a mug of something potent. One particularly
disgusting brew was made from mangel-wurzels. I
do remember having particularly good compost that year.

it might come in handy…

My father is capable of making anything from a piece or metal or wood and can fix objects others would have long since parted with. He is incapable of throwing out anything which "might come in handy," and as a result, has the largest collection of nails, screws, springs, and brackets in the world. The only problem is, he will never purchase anything, so when a particular type of screw is required for a job likely to take seconds, he will spend two days searching through old tobacco tins until he has discovered that the one type of screw he hasn't got is the one needed for the job. In despair after witnessing the umpteenth bi-annual week long screw sorting ceremony on the kitchen table, my daughter was persuaded, since it was not deemed tactful for anyone else to do it, to buy him sets of plastic screw boxes with clear fronts for all birthdays and Christmases, so he could sort them once and for all. Pronounced the best presents ever, we speculated on how many months could have been saved had we thought of it sooner. He still never has the right screw, but it only takes two hours instead of two days now to discover the fact.

There is nothing so time wasting as searching for things you know you have. I always think that money and time are well spent on the acquisition, or creation, or decent storage units. Wall racks for large tools mean you can actually get into the shed and avoid the rake treading antics that farces thrive on. Plastic boxes for wire and string, another for galvanized nails, and so on. Anything which is placed on the floor will rarely be put away later and if we can get into the habit of keeping things tidy as we work, we can save a lot of precious time and effort. Boxes need labels and the adhesive paper variety will inevitably drop off the boxes in the winter damp. Permanent markers are the only solution for shed storage boxes. I recently came across an unlabeled box which rattled alarmingly. Inside were crushed eggshells. I had only a vague recall of washing out used shells the year before and crunching them up to discourage slugs and snails from attacking my seedlings, but they had suffered damage for yet another season and all for want of a label.

I have never been able to figure out the practice of placing the garden shed at the furthest possible point from the house, hidden away in the undergrowth. The fact is that if you have got five minutes to spare which could be put to productive use, you are less likely to use it if you have to walk a long way to get the shears from the shed. You may have to walk across damp grass or on soil, so you will need to change your shoes. You will need to find the key, because since the shed is in a remote position you will probably keep it locked at all times. By the time you have thought about all this, you will probably decide not to bother after all. If the shed is close to the house you are much more likely to put small amount of available time to good use and will probably keep it tidier too.

Practice random acts
of kindness and
senseless acts
of beauty.

Anon.

Competition

The world is a competitive place, and while we usually think of gardens as tranquil places, there is often a great deal of competitive spirit lurking there too. The obvious example is The Chelsea Flower Show, in England, where competition is fierce among designers to have their designs accepted, to win a medal, and, of course, to win the coveted "Best Garden" award. At Chelsea, as at many horticultural shows, individual growers have their chance to display flowers and crops they have nurtured to as near perfection as they can make them. Occasionally, the competition is less than healthy and rivalry kicks in to the point where exhibits are sabotaged. I often wonder at the purpose of such intensity. The achievement is in participating and in the satisfaction that you have done your best.

the best plot

Competition can take away the pleasure of gardening. Each year, my allotment society has a "Best Plot" competition. Most people just do what they do anyway, but others take it very seriously. The plots on either side of mine are immaculate and their owners, being, on one side, retired and the other, redundant, spend an incredible amount of time there.

The man on the right comments loudly to others on my frequent misdemeanors—growing nettles, for example. I do in fairness harvest all the dandelion heads and cut down all the annual grasses before they drift his way and am obsessional in my edging of the grass border on his side. Because of the tension, however, I am reluctant to go to the plot when he is there and have often been known to drive past if I see his car.

On the other side is an eighty-year-old, who has had several near misses but labors on undaunted. If I see his car, I always go in just to chat, even if I am not planning to stay and work. His attitude is that I am busy and do what I can when I can. If things get out of hand on his side, he will lay cardboard or plastic on my weeds which helps us both. He offers me beans and I offer him whatever I have available. He ties up my fallen artichokes and I tie up his fruit cage netting to keep the pigeons out. It works well and is effort well spent.

formulas

for the garden

Books and formulas do not create a garden, but we all need to take guidance and can learn much from the experience and ideas of others. Ancient formulas, yin and yang, and the five elements are merely a way of looking at an environment in order to gauge if it is balanced. Sometimes when I look at gardens, I will mumble "Too metal," which for me means—too still, too white, too heavy, too round, and in need of some support from other colors or shapes to balance it. I wouldn't dream of putting a fire color next to an earth color, next to a metal color just because that is the way the formula is written in books, any more than you would ever see it like that in an Eastern garden or in the natural world.

who
what
where
how
why
when

?

Asking specific questions about the design of the garden, or about each task you undertake there, is a workable formula. The Who-What-Where-How-Why-When formula can help ensure that we have considered all the options and are likely to carry out each task efficiently.

who
what
where
how
why
when

Who will be using the garden? This may seem an obvious question, but each family member may have a different ideas about how they will use the garden.

When you look in magazines and books for ideas, you will notice that children are rarely catered for, since children's play areas do rather mess up a design. First of all, when children are young, they need to be within sight, which usually means that the terrace area is usually covered with sand and toys. There will need to be a soft landing area under swings and climbing frames and these are not usually picturesque. Children grow up quickly, and will soon need places to kick a ball, which will have implications for windows and plants. Later, they will need secret areas to do things children do when they think they are not being observed. Ponds and pools have implications for children and have to be planned with safety in mind. Children grow up and move on, but, before you know it, will return with their own children in tow.

You will need quiet places to relax, to carry out hobbies, and to entertain. Will your terrace cope with the numbers you plan to invite for dinner and will you have enough informal seating for impromptu gatherings? If we are aware of likely uses of the garden initially, we can position the sandpit to change into a flower bed later, and the climbing frame area into a workshop when we have more time to pursue our hobbies, without causing major upheaval each time.

who

what

where

how

why

when

What features you decide to have in your garden determines the design. Just as it is well to be aware right from the start whether you are likely to acquire two more cars in a year or two when the children are older, so it is to be aware of where you are going to keep the sunbeds, and so on.

Ponds are fashionable at the moment, but they are high maintenance if they are not to become clogged and smelly. In an open space, they attract feathered visitors lured by the fish. In shady places, the algae seem to colonize with alarming speed. Where they are overhung with deciduous trees, you will have problems in the autumn.

Vegetables and fruit have specific demands on space and paths, and if not carefully planned, can be inadequate for your needs. It pays to look at the plants you choose in terms of their usefulness to the design, to surrounding plants, and to your lifestyle, some being far higher maintenance than others.

who
what
where
how
why
when

Where you place the features is quite crucial if we are to save time and effort on unnecessary tasks because we have failed to account for how the different functions of the garden work together. Getting the flow right and seeing the connections between various components and their users and uses initially can save problems later. There is no point placing a herb bed at the far end of the garden if you use it several times a day in meal preparation. Right by the kitchen door is the best place for it, to save time and to ensure that meals are as tasty as they can be. There are other food crops which are best close by. Salad leaves are fast growing and soon run to seed, and a ready supply sown among other plants in the flower beds not only adds interest but is also functional. Those items we have far less dealings with—rhubarb, fruit trees, and bushes—can be positioned away from the immediate vicinity of the house, although it is as good to plan the garden so that you can benefit from the fruit blossom in the spring.

Although we might not want the main compost bins right by the back door, we are more likely to recycle kitchen waste if we have a temporary store there which we can empty into the main bin once a week. Otherwise we might be tempted just to throw it out with the trash. We can also make use of our knowledge of how plants grow and support each other naturally and plant in a similar way. An idea worth investigation is "Forest Gardening," which takes into account the way in which trees and other plants support each other in a natural environment. Those who practice Forest Gardening find natural ways of integrating decorative and food plants in low maintenance supportive environments.

who
what
where
how
why
when

How we do things is important if we want to save time, effort, and planning. Seeing the whole picture and the effects of our actions can be crucial. When making the compost area, for example, we need more than one bin. Otherwise what will we do with the material waiting to be composted? Smaller receptacles are useful to sort the materials until they can be mixed together in the final heap, plus we need to build in space to turn out the compost when it is ready. It always seems a shame to waste the fertile soil around the bins; rhubarb and squashes will thrive there and help to mask the bins.

who
what
where
how
why
when

Our gardens seem to fill up with plants effortlessly however we come by them, but it is useful to ask ourselves why we select them. A plant may be pretty, but it can also be beneficial to other plants around it. It might add to the salad bowl, smell pleasant, or provide twigs to stake other plants. Will the birds be able to make use of the seed it produces and will it attract pollinating insects into the garden to help the vegetable crop? Do we need to buy comparatively expensive bean poles when the stout stems of jerusalem artichokes will serve us well the following season, provide an interesting addition to our diet, and feed the compost heap thereafter?

who

what

where

how

why

when

"Nature is
what takes over
when the gardener
turns his or
her back."

Abby Adams

permaculture

A modern movement which can offer ideas to put our effort to best use in the garden is called "permaculture," a system for living devised by Australians Bill Mollison and David Holmgren, as a result of the loss of biodiversity in Mollison's native Tasmania. The word is a contraction of **perma**nent agri**culture**, but also of the notion of permanent culture since they felt that it is not possible for societies to survive without an ethical base for sustainable practices on the land. Mollison's aim was "to create systems that are ecologically sound and economically viable, which provide for their own needs, do not exploit or pollute, and are therefore sustainable in the long term." It is very much an up to date version of the ancient art of feng shui, which emanated from ancient China and has become popular in the West. Like feng shui, permaculture is based on the observation of how people and landscapes work together, and how modern science and technology can play their part in creating an ecology which works in the modern world. It is a philosophy based on working with, rather than against, nature and can offer many ideas for reducing unnecessary work in the garden and putting our labors to productive use.

Permaculture—Summary

The Goal
- Be absolutely sure what your aim is

Design
- Create things which will save time and effort, not increase it
- Introduce elements which can fulfil more than one function

Planning
- Plan long- and short-term goals meticulously
- Plan for most used elements near the house and least used furthest away
- Consider the effects of each action

Cooperation
- Work with other gardeners to share plants and produce
- Sell your produce locally or exchange it for services required
- Recycle unwanted materials
- Install water butts for rain and bath water
- Conserve energy and install alternative methods where possible

Progress
- Make sure you have the correct tools and materials available before you start

Work Flow
- Position materials in the order you will need them where they will not need to be moved again
- Finish one job at a time and clear everything away when completed

Tutors and books, the Internet and formulas make useful guides, and the ideas they offer can save us a great deal of effort when we set out to create a garden, but there is absolutely no substitute for getting your hands dirty and becoming familiar with the nature of the plants and materials you work with and the rhythms of the yearly cycle. "Experience is the best of schoolmates, only the school fees are heavy," wrote Thomas Carlyle. With the right thought, we can get a discount.

...gardens are not made by singing ...
"oh how beautiful" and sitting in the shade.

Rudyard Kipling

chapter 4

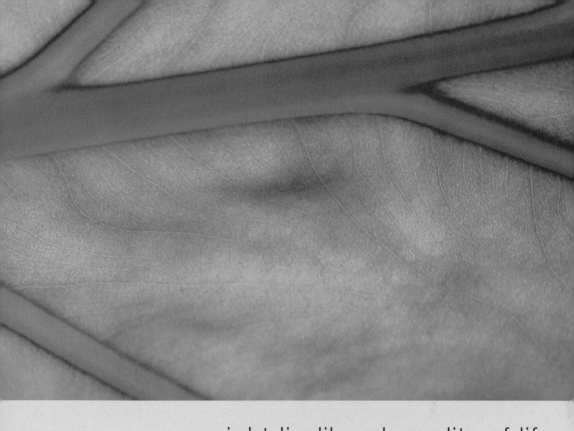

right livelihood: quality of life

"Life in the modern city has become a symbol of the fact that man can become adapted to starless

skies, treeless avenues, shapeless buildings, tasteless bread, joyless celebration, spiritless pleasures."

Rene Dubos

As a Western society, we have never been so fortunate in terms of health and wealth, but happiness still eludes us, when listening to the news or reading newspapers, or even talking to friends, it is rare to find anyone who will admit to being truly happy. It seems that the more we gain in material terms, the less contented we are with our lot. Some of the most contented are those who love gardening. Tending a garden, however small, can be our art, our poetry, our creativity, and our joy. We do not have to pay thousands of dollars for a painting or a sculpture. Instead, we can merely break off a shoot and plant it, and by the following year it will have given birth to something wonderful that will be our legacy. Where else in life can we achieve so much, so simply?

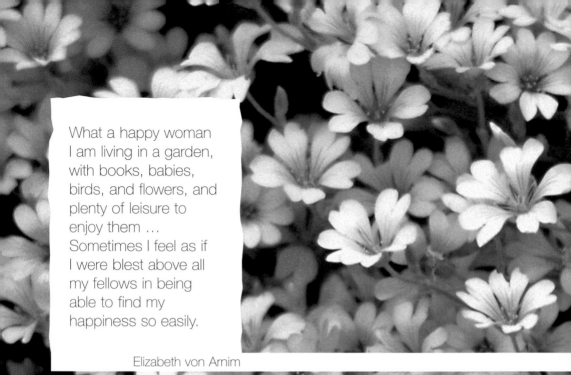

What a happy woman
I am living in a garden,
with books, babies,
birds, and flowers, and
plenty of leisure to
enjoy them …
Sometimes I feel as if
I were blest above all
my fellows in being
able to find my
happiness so easily.

Elizabeth von Arnim

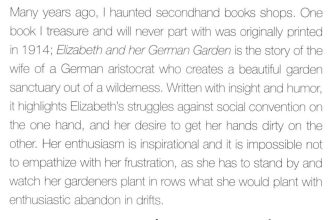

Many years ago, I haunted secondhand books shops. One book I treasure and will never part with was originally printed in 1914; *Elizabeth and her German Garden* is the story of the wife of a German aristocrat who creates a beautiful garden sanctuary out of a wilderness. Written with insight and humor, it highlights Elizabeth's struggles against social convention on the one hand, and her desire to get her hands dirty on the other. Her enthusiasm is inspirational and it is impossible not to empathize with her frustration, as she has to stand by and watch her gardeners plant in rows what she would plant with enthusiastic abandon in drifts.

euphoria

We all need inspiration from time to time and to know we are on the right path. I needed to find the book when I did, and would recommend it to anyone looking for a book on gardening, as it offers a journey through ignorance and excitement, joys and disappointments, and expresses the sheer enthusiasm of a passionate gardener.

passion

Watching a gardener doubled over wrestling with wet wind-blown leaves, or mud-covered and red-cheeked maneuvering an over-laden barrow of manure across a boggy lawn, it is understandable that the word "gardener" does not immediately conjure up grace, beauty, and passion to a layman's eye. Yet observe a gardener lift a tiny fuschia flower and peer into its depths for a full five minutes, cup a ripe peach warmed by the afternoon sun in their hands, and sink their nose into the velvet petals of the damask rose and just believe that gardeners are the most passionate people on earth.

"What you burden
yourselves with
through your thoughts
words or deeds can
be redeemed by no
one but yourselves …

Therefore free yourselves.

Abd-Ru-Shin

letting go

When we move towards a Zen lifestyle, we decide what is important in life and what we have no need of. The *I Ching* suggests that:

"Even with slender means,
the sentiment of the heart can be expressed."

Fear of how others see us and of how we will provide for ourselves and our family can make life in the present very sterile. However much we plan, life has a habit of introducing elements to change our expectations. The quality of our lives now is important. Buddhists believe that cravings are the origins of all human suffering.

"Love your neighbor,
yet pull not down
your hedge."

George Herbert—Outlandish Proverbs, 1640

barriers

We were burgled once and immediately afterwards I removed all the barriers around the house, so that any burglar mad enough to embark on a wild goose chase again would be seen by all the neighbors. Plants help me at the vulnerable spots which cannot be seen—pyracantha and holly make the best alarm systems, created by the burglars themselves when the thorns get them, and no burglar in his right mind is going to leap through a tangle of clematis montana into a manure heap.

Soon after the spate of local burglaries, weeding behind a bush in the front garden, I listened unobserved as three local lads went by. One was explaining to the others where the best pickings were—the latest computers at one house, AV equipment at another, and jewelery and spare cash somewhere else. They walked straight past my house in disgust.

My best collection is in the garden and of no interest to anyone but me. William Morris wrote that a garden "should be well fenced from the outside world." Robert Frost, in his poem "Mending Wall," suggested that "Good fences make good neighbors," which is a sentiment I prefer, though dependent on your understanding of the word "good." Yapping dogs, couch, and bindweed are not the most pleasant things to offer others and good fences or barriers can ensure that all is tranquil in the neighborhood.

the cottage

One of the saddest sights I have seen is the fate of a little cottage perched on top of the South Downs in Sussex. Through its long history it must have had stunning views across the countryside from the garden and from the kitchen window. A new house was built eight years ago between it and the view to its south, and the vitality of the little cottage is slowly seeping away. A wall of conifers, fifteen feet high and growing, blocks the view and the light. Standing on tip toes in an upstairs window, it might just be possible to see beyond the trees, but only for another year or two. The conifers are not in keeping with what remains of the ancient woodland which crowns the hill, and from a distance appear to be a thoughtless blot on the landscape. Respect for others and for the landscape is such a little thing.

"I feel sorry for plants that are obliged to make a struggle for life in uncongenial situations because their owner wishes all things."

Elizabeth von Arnim

struggle

Plants have certain needs. Some plants are acid lovers and others prefer an alkaline soil. Some like dry conditions and others like shade. Some plants originated in mountainous regions where the soil is shallow and gritty, and others will have benefited from the deep humus of woodland. If we attempt to grow plants in conditions which are unnatural for them, or in soils which they would not naturally choose, we have a struggle on our hands to keep them healthy. I have read that if you replace soil in a bed, say remove alkaline soil and replace it with acid, that you can grow azaleas, but over time, the rain and the earthworms move the soil downwards and the chalk and alkaline rock from below filters throughout it. It would be much better to move to another area to fulfil your dreams or go with the flow where you are.

freedom

Within the past few years there has been a radical change in the way we stake plants. Previously, it was always recommended to plant trees and standard shrubs next to a tall stake and strap them bolt upright to it. It has recently been discovered that the trunks and stems of unstaked plants increase their girth much faster simply because they can move around, and thus they become sturdier, healthy plants, with no obvious bend or lean, since it is in a plant's own nature to grow straight upwards unless an obstacle prevents it. It is now recommended that tall plants should be anchored across the root ball so that they stay firm in the ground, letting their leaves and branches roam free.

air

Plants, like people, need air and the freedom to be themselves. In a tangled border, we cannot appreciate the individual forms of each plant, and we risk the plant diseases associated with overcrowding and competition for water and nutrients. By planting as naturally as we can in mixed beds, we may help prevent an increase in disease and the need for chemical control, and thus avoid a dependency cycle.

We are always advised to plant wall trained plants at least twelve inches from the base of a wall, since the bricks, being porous, use up most of the moisture. I would advocate increasing this distance to allow the free flow of air behind as well as in front of the plants, to reduce the risk of fungal diseases.

the three sisters

A Native American custom is to plant beans next to corn so they can use the straight stem to coil around. Underneath, they plant squash, so that the broad leaves can shade the roots of the other plants and keep weeds at bay. They call this mutually supportive system "The Three Sisters," and it is copied widely in organic gardening circles around the world. Visitors to the Greek Islands will still witness the practice of growing garlic under fruit trees to ward off pests. It works well under roses too.

support

What our ancestors intuitively knew about the benefits of growing plants which support each other, modern science can prove. When plant sap is put through a chemical process, it forms a pattern, or a "signature" and each plant has its own distinctive pattern. The sap of plants which benefit each other have patterns which are harmonious, while those which do not repel each other.

system

Some plants store minerals and make them available to plants around them by root secretions. Others lure pollinating insects by their smell or color, for the benefit of plants nearby. Some plants repel pests, or act as sacrificial plants to lure pests away from other plants. Birds are attracted to plants offering them seed and moisture and may be encouraged to make a meal of the aphids nearby on a neighbor. There are some herbs which act as a soil disinfectant, keeping fungal diseases at bay. Some of the benefits of planting certain types of plants together are obvious to us, but others we can learn only by observation. Many a child's knee, stung by nettles, has been soothed by the application of a dock leaf; docks and nettles are a classic example of companion planting. The large tap root of the dock breaks up compacted soil to enable the nettle roots to push through and they, in turn, put the heart back into it and create mineral-rich black loam.

sweet scented

Leaves on fine leafed plant—the curry plant, fennel, and wormwood—have a greater leaf area than that, say, of sorrel, which has large broad leaves. There is always a purpose in nature. Look at the quality of the fine leafed plants. They are known for their smell. The more surface area, the more smell. When planning a herb garden, bear this in mind. If you put all your smelly plants into one bed, their smells will cancel each other out, confusing you and also the insects attracted to them. It is likely that the overload will be too much for the weakest of them and they will take themselves off and seed themselves into more congenial places, or make their way to the compost heap exhausted by the competition.

good
balance

When a plant has grown in the same place for a long time, it will have removed all the nutrients it needs from the soil. We replace this as best we can by adding compost and manure to redress the balance. Like people, most plants have a life span and pass on when their energy is exhausted and a likely cause will be the depletion of the substances they require in the soil. If a plant or part of a hedge dies and you attempt to replace it with another plant of the same family, the chances are it will not survive and if it does, it will not thrive. We need to be aware of the needs of plants and observe the conditions they enjoy.

Crop rotation is not practiced as widely as it was in the past because a large part of the world's agriculture is dependent on the addition of minerals in powdered form. In the past, farmers and gardeners moved their crops around to different positions each year, knowing which crops were beneficial to those following or preceding them. Rotation of plants in the garden can help prevent a buildup of the diseases and pests which normally attack a particular family of plants and prevent the depletion of a specific nutrient from the soil. It is therefore important to have plant knowledge, since often it is not immediately obvious which plants belong to the same family. If we plant cabbages, followed by kohlrabi, followed by radish, followed by a green manure of mustard, we would be using plants from the same family each time. Three or four years in the rotation cycle are most common, but that recommended by the Biodynamic movement based on a fivefold rotation makes the most sense. There are five parts to a plant—leaf, root, seed, flower, and fruit. The fivefold rotation takes into account that a particular plant organ will also have some impact on the types of nutrients removed and put back into the soil. I make sure that I include something of each of the five plant parts in the compost heap to give it balance, although it is best not to include some seeds and roots, of the most pernicious weeds, in case the composting process does not break them down completely.

fivefold rotation

companion
planting

The following list is not comprehensive but includes examples of the more commonly known companions of widely available plants. You will add to the list as you become more familiar with your garden. Where there is no other obvious cause for a plant's distress, the mere fact that they are not keen on their neighbors might be the reason that they are not looking too well.

	Like	Dislike
Apples	Garlic, Chives	Carrots, Potatoes
Apricots	Nasturtiums, Basil	Tomatoes, Southernwood
Beans	Marigolds, Petunias	Sunflowers, Onions
Brassicas	Pansies, Lavender	Rue, Vines
Cucumbers	Borage, Yarrow	Marjoram, Thyme
Lettuce	Currants, Strawberries	Fennel, Rue
Onions	Chamomile, Parsley	Asparagus, Marjoram
Peas	Mint, Sweetcorn	Horseradish, Leeks
Potatoes	Foxgloves, Tagetes	Raspberries, Orache
Squashes	Borage, Fennel	Rosemary, Sage
Tomatoes	Lemon Balm, Roses	Caraway, Wormwood

guardian of the garden

Our gardens can improve our quality of life and we in return owe it to the plants to ensure that we provide them with the best conditions we can. By being aware of their needs and following the natural way, we can create a healthy lifestyle for ourselves and our surroundings.

chapter 5

right speech: expression

Meditation: "The Earth has music for those who will listen." William Shakespeare

Zen encourages us to express ourselves openly and confidently. The act of becoming self-conscious about what we are doing will cause us to lose sight of our original purpose and color what we set out to achieve. Our path will remain focused, but this will not be at the expense of others. Zen teaches compassion and love, and if we find enjoyment in our lives we have no need to seek a reward.

the right focus

As the world moves towards globalization, style in design, both interior and exterior, has taken on an international look. Large multinational companies dictate "the look" in our sitting rooms and which plants we can grow in our gardens, and it is possible to sit in a hotel room anywhere in the world with little to indicate which continent you are on.

It is easy to remain in the past and lament an idyllic lost culture, a dream which has little place in reality. It is easy too to embrace each new craze as it hits the fashion magazines and lose our sense of identity and the spirit of the place in which we live. We are possibly less free than we ever were to express our individuality. In a Zen garden, we can retain our own focus and express ourselves freely while retaining the integrity of the place in which we live.

no ego trip

"Ego-soul is the seed of birth and death,
And the foolish call it the true man."

Zuigan

If freedom is living and working within a natural environment, with the opportunity to express yourself as you wish, then can there be a better point to life? Unfortunately, society is organized in such a way that, short of opting out of things completely, it is difficult to live this kind of lifestyle.

It is possible to live a Zen lifestyle without having to opt out of life or move and leave friends and family. What matters is how we express ourselves in all we do and in the way we think. A Zen lifestyle is to do your work quietly and humbly and to let go of the negative emotions which may accompany the process.

tradition and heritage

No topic in any of the arts—and good gardening is definitely an art—is so hotly debated as that of preserving tradition and heritage. The global look may just be a fad, but there are many who lament it. John Makepeace at Parnham College of Furniture in Dorset, England, whose students produce some of the finest pieces of high quality furniture on the market today, expresses, "We have a special landscape, and our materials and design should communicate a sense of who we are," a comment applicable anywhere in the world. Pieces produced by the students are not just copies of designs from the past, they are innovative and individual, while retaining the spirit of their country and its style.

It is the same with gardens. Ancient gardens were not only built to the same geometric proportions which govern everything in the universe, but they also incorporated materials and plants which were indigenous to the region, or which were known to survive the conditions of the places in which they were used. This gives gardens a certain spiritual quality linking them to their immediate environment and to the larger universe. In losing the larger picture, we lose something of the quality of each garden. There are reasons for a national style. Availability of materials is one. Another is the quality of the light. Deep, vibrant Mediterranean colors look well in the bright blue light of their origin and out of place in the grey light of a British winter. Plants too have their place.

"A foolish consistency is the hobgoblin of little minds.
With consistency, a great soul has nothing to do."

Ralph Waldo Emerson

community spirit

There are reasons why we should remain true to the spirit of the locality in which we live. Globalization has created a situation where food is transported around the world, enabling us to partake of any cuisine we choose. However, one of the best pieces of advice for the preservation of world resources I ever heard was from William Spear, who suggested that our aim should be to eat only "what you can catch and what you can grow." In the past, each family would have a small piece of land and grow their own food and perhaps keep a few chickens. If they also worked on a large estate, they would be offered rabbits, venison, pheasants caught at the hunt, and those with an eye to the main chance would probably poach a few for good measure. By and large all food was grown and produced locally and people ate in season that which was available. Nowadays we are encouraged to eat locally grown food from the organic lobby who are keen to preserve the quality of food as well as support local production.

We may think ourselves fortunate to have so much choice in the Western world, but there has been some research recently, by Dr. Paavo Airolo, to show that perhaps it would be better to give a corner of our gardens over to growing at least some of our food, or at least ensuring that it is as local and fresh as it can be. Healthy soil contains penicillin fungi which will have developed and regulated themselves in each environment in order to be able to see off the bacteria also present in each location. Since we live in the same location as these penicillin fungi in our gardens, with regard to the air, soil, and water, it follows that we can benefit from the fungi actions in our soil. Therefore in eating produce from our own gardens, we will be receiving a healthier diet than if we eat food artificially produced which offers no resistance to the diseases and ailments which might befall us.

respect where

you dwell

Lao Tzu suggests that "awful things will happen" to those who do not respect nature. Indeed, the Eastern belief is that the earth has energy channels, and if they are punctured in the wrong place then trouble will follow; in the same way, practitioners of acupuncture use needles to unblock chi from the energy channels in the body. The scientific language of the West sometimes finds it hard to accommodate this view. There are conditions that we create, however, which could be avoided if we just stand back and apply logic. Every now and again, a newspaper will report that a house or garden has disappeared into a hole. It will later be discovered that the houses have been built on the site of a mine shaft and the earth has given way. When we damage the face of a hill or mountain, we cut across the natural water channels which carry the rain down the mountain, and in doing so, divert the water who knows where, to flood someone's land perhaps. We certainly cut through the ancient animal tracks when we build motorways through a landscape and divide communities in half, destroying the community spirit which had evolved over centuries.

In the garden we need to be aware of our actions when we undertake construction work. With water features and ponds so popular, we may be inclined to divert streams to feed our ponds or to make them more accessible to us when we sit on the terrace. When we do this, we will possibly not think about the affect on the wildlife. When we dam a stream, all the plants and wildlife below the dam are now without water. Where will the excess water above end up? When we build extensions to our houses, we may cut through the roots of established trees. We could be creating problems for ourselves, since, in heavy winds, with no anchorage, the trees could topple onto our new construction.

joyce's garden

I have a friend who lives by the coast, not in a picturesque tourist spot—on account of its rather unappealing stone and seaweed beach, its exposure to the extremes of the inclement blustery wind, and its lack of access and amenities. As gardens go, Joyce's is almost brutal, but as such, it is a perfect expression of where it is. All that divides it from the sea is a low eighteen-inch wall, scarcely visible among the valerian plants which form the bulk of the planting in the garden and on the vast sweep of the stone and shingle beach beyond. The wall marks a boundary that is both insignificance and powerlessness against the might of the crashing surf beyond. It is a stark but strangely beautiful place and the only attempt made to humanize it is a mermaid, made from driftwood and other ocean debris, sitting on a rock and gazing wistfully out to sea. Her contrasting delicate presence excentuates the sheer power and might of the elements and the winter waves that encroach upon the perimeter garden wall.

Gazing across at other gardens along the beach, I can only respect my friend Joyce's acknowledgement of, and sense of, place. The sheer power of the natural environment overshadows and overwhelms the attempts of those who struggle to maintain lawns or keep alive plants more suited to gentler environments inland and reminds us, forcibly at times, that though we strive to impose our will and tame the natural world, we can never match its magnificence and strength.

personalities

"Everything in life is speaking, is audible,
is communicating, in spite of its apparent silence."

Hazrat Inayat Khan

No two gardens can ever be the same, each the personal expression of its creator. There are those we see along the way which are similar to all the others along the way—the place between us and the pavement, or the place where the children kick a ball in summer. These gardens we tend not to see as we move from one place to another. Those which catch our attention are those created with care, where a special plant or a fine border catch our eye, or a cleverly placed sculpture, or a simple willow figure. These places are those with a spirit, brought to life by the attention of their owner's unique expression.

drunk on roses

Ji Cheng in the *Yuan Ye*, or *The Craft of Gardens*, written in 1631, suggested that roses should never be tied up, but allowed to grow freely, because when they are tied back and heavily pruned they are unlikely to remain undamaged.

For Vita Sackville-West, creator of the world famous gardens at Sissinghurst in Kent, it is possible to be "drunk on roses." I have always viewed them as watered-down squash, which neither quenches the thirst nor elates the senses. I suppose I have never tried the real thing, those allowed to scramble free through trees, which escape the snip and chop of human action. I inherited a bed of roses in my first garden and did not enjoy the experience of dealing with black spot, mildew, and aphids which followed one another with tedious regularity, so I have never bothered with them since.

We should not blame the roses, of course. They have been overbred, and as a result, together with rigorous pruning programs that we are urged to employ, roses are feeble things, prone to every illness and pest attack. A rose bed can often seem lifeless; the roses stand in rows, with nothing to balance them. Perhaps if we treated them as we do other plants and let them go their own way, they would be more appealing. Vita Sackville-West suggested "I hate to see things scrimp and scrubby and I would now suggest that you should try the experiment of not slaughtering your roses…"

a roof of irises

> "It is pleasant to know each of your plants intimately because you have chosen and placed every one of them. In the course of time, they become real friends, conjuring up pleasant associations of the people who gave them and the gardens they came from."
>
> Elizabeth von Arnim

We often plant things—roses usually, but occasionally trees and other shrubs—to commemorate someone who has died. A very dear friend of the family died a few years ago. She was a long time passing and we all suffered in the waiting. While she was visiting, I planted a clematis called "Edith" in my garden and our friend was delighted and asked after it regularly, knowing, that when she was gone, every day, for a few weeks a year, the translucent glow of the petals would shine out from the shrubbery and keep her memory alive, while we would not mourn or forget, but delight in her presence.

Visiting one garden I found a thatched gazebo with irises growing from the roof. The story was that they and some friends had often planned to retire to a cottage in Normandy, a place where their families had spent many happy holidays. The friends had achieved it, but they knew that they would never make it. To remind them of the fun they had, they copied the old Normandy custom of planting irises on thatch to bind it together and to give a wonderful show in summer.

"It is the marriage of the soul with nature that makes the intellect fruitful and gives birth to the imagination."

Henry James Thoreau

expression

Until quite recently, gardening advice has made its way into the public domain via experts and journals which are part of the gardening "establishment." "Advice," Helen Yem, a garden designer, was heard to suggest, "for the horticulturally challenged by the spatially privileged." There is now a new breed of gardening journal catering for those enthusiasts who may have just a tiny balcony on which to commune with nature, and full of inspirational ideas and sound advice. There have always been those who stand out, not because of their grand plans or because of their vast knowledge, but because of their individual approach, their enthusiasm, and their willingness to try something new.

inspirational

gardens

Those who strike out and go their own way often do so at the risk of isolation from their peers. Inevitably they will attract comment, favorable or not, and often this takes courage, but they seem to pursue their own path regardless, and how richer we all are for it. As interest in gardening grows, we are privileged to be able to peep into the private gardens of some great artists through the pages of books, but better still by experiencing them firsthand.

if a job's worth doing…

…do it well and do it now. Having just visited a newly built, very expensive house, where it was not possible to place even a single bed in one of the bedrooms or for anyone over 5'8" tall weighing more than 130 pounds to get into one of the shower cubicles and close the door, it brought home to me that what makes the old more desirable than the new is its durability and quality and the skills of the people who built and made things. We appreciate what we achieve much more if we strive for quality and if we do a job well. When it is finished, we can let it go and move on to the next job, otherwise it will come back to haunt us later.

At one point, my father's garage housed four lawn mowers, one working and three waiting to be mended. A conspiracy by persons unknown spirited away three to the local dump. It took him two years to realize, but he quickly filled up the space they left. Where it is possible to mend broken objects, the time to do it is now. Tomorrow will be too late and they will have become clutter in the shed and in the mind.

topiary

Garden centers are full of topiary. Box balls and pyramids rub shoulders with conifers fashioned into pom poms. I have even seen bicycles and tables ready to be transported to a terrace or front porch. In the East, the art of bonsai is a similar attempt to fashion nature, but there the desire is to make it a perfect representation of its form in the natural world, rather than the desire to somehow mold nature into unnatural shapes for our amusement. There is also a distinction to be made between those who purchase a piece of topiary much as they would an urn to decorate their garden and someone who has devoted many years to the painstaking task of learning the growth habits of a plant and meticulously creating something from it over many years—the Zen approach.

ornament

There have always been ornaments in gardens—from the simplest ancient pot to an expensive modern sculpture, since our gardens are places in which we can express ourselves freely, unencumbered by convention as we often are indoors.

Sculpture gardens are popular worldwide. Artists can explore the power of a natural backdrop for creations in stone, steel, willow, and wood and we can experience the form and texture of the materials. In private gardens, individuals express themselves in a thousand different ways—for example, the sheer magic and detail of Margot Knox's Mosaic Garden in Melbourne, Australia, which is reminiscent of Gaudi's park benches in Barcelona. Ivan Hick's surreal garden at Stansted Park, where the legs emerging from a canoe and the door in the trees serves to intrigue and interest.

We can visit and marvel at the work of others and find inspiration from it, but nothing can replace the things we have created ourselves in our own space.

the language of trees

Because Zen Buddhism comes from the East, it is natural to look East and to try to adopt their symbolism and images, mainly because they have been preserved in the daily lives and thoughts of peoples in the East over the centuries. Similar traditions existed in the West, although the language used reflected the natural world and lifestyles of those living there.

The Celts, who inhabited Britain and parts of northern Europe, like their Eastern counterparts, lived in harmony with their natural environments and believed that the spirit behind creation was in all things. They were tuned in to the particular properties and qualities of each tree and plant, and this knowledge was handed down each generation by wise elders and poets. Poetry held the secret key to the secrets of the universe and was respected and revered. The Druids spoke in the language of trees and plants to communicate their wisdom. There were various types of ogham language, the ogham of trees and of birds being just two. Britain was covered by forests in those days at which time the ogham of trees became a powerful means of communication among the wise and knowledgeable. Each tree became synonymous with the alphabet, direction, months of the year, and a host of other correspondences, including those pertaining to health, much like the associations of the five elements in the East.

finding

the path to

self-expression

There is room for us to express our individuality in the garden, not by imposing our will upon it as a dominant force, but by working with the intrinsic nature of the plants and materials we find there. Dogen suggested that undertaking an activity is not a guarantee that we will gain anything from it unless we are ready to. The Zen way is to quietly go about our business with the flow of the natural world, doing what we have to do.

chapter 6

right concentration: tasks

Meditation: "To the mind that is still, the whole universe surrenders." Lao Tzu

There are few who have gardens so remote that nothing of the outside world impinges on them. Traffic noise, airplanes, the smells from the local factory, tomorrow's trip, this morning's disagreement—all these things accompany us in what we would consider our tranquil space. To remove all external stimuli is beyond our control, but we can still the mind so that it is not aware of anything outside what we are doing at this precise moment. When we can do this, we will no longer be so affected by the everyday things which take up our time and clog up our minds. To be able to still the mind is a gift, which, when we receive it, surpasses all others. It is a gift we give to ourselves. When we receive the gift we will be able to undertake each task efficiently and give it our full concentration. When it is over, we will be able to move on to the next one.

the ant

One day, sitting on the back step, I witnessed a drama unfolding before my eyes. At the foot of a wall there seemed to be a battle raging, as a tiny ant grappled with an enormous wasp— and seemed to be winning. It appeared to have stunned the wasp in some way, who, although struggling to free itself, did not seem to be able to move its wings and escape. All sorts of questions went through my mind. How did the ant stun the wasp? Why didn't the wasp sting the ant? And how had the ant disabled the wasp's wings? Slowly the questions, to which there were no answers, began to fade and I became intent on just watching. When eventually the telephone rang, I did not want to leave, but reluctantly dragged myself away. When I returned the drama was over—they had gone.

and the wasp

I read somewhere that "Concentration is not to try too hard to watch something" and certainly, if you become involved in a situation such as that between the ant and the wasp, the questions flow and the mind works relentlessly. Suzuki says that you should not attempt to calm the mind, because in doing so you will not be achieving the right kind of concentration. "Stop thinking meditation is anything special," says Surya Singer, "Stop thinking altogether." If we sit somewhere long enough, we can become detached and just observe the situation as it is and not attach our own ideas and logic to it. When we do this, we create our own reality, not see it as it is. If we consciously try to meditate, we will be unable to relax enough to achieve it. Where we develop the right kind of concentration, we are able to detach from our thoughts and surroundings and just sit, or concentrate on the task we are doing.

"When you do
something, you
should do it with
your whole body
and mind;
you should be
concentrated on
what you do."

Suzuki

a juggling act

Women often pride themselves on the ability to be able to undertake several tasks at the same time, and are often heard to suggest that this makes them in some way superior to men. I used to think that "Killing two birds with one stone," or even more if it could be managed, was a virtue, but now I am less convinced. I am not talking about the Permaculture idea of utilizing objects which can fulfil more than one purpose, but the notion that we can juggle lots of balls at the same time. It is very easy to get sidetracked in the garden. No sooner do you start pruning a bush, then you notice that a climber needs tying in, or a pot has fallen over, and you go to sort them out. While doing this, you notice a host of other things, and by the time you return to the pruning, it will probably be time to pack up for the day. The Zen way is to concentrate on what you are doing and complete the task before moving on to the next.

Look at the battle you are involved in;

you are caught in it:

you are it.

Krishnamurti

recycling

It might be suggested that rummaging through dumpsters is not a Zen activity. It is and it isn't—it depends on the motive. When I acquired my allotment, I needed compost bins. Being in an open public place, it is not advisable to leave anything of value on an allotment, so the purchase of new plastic bins was not a viable solution. Having spied two wooden pallets outside a house nearby, I decided I had hit on the solution. I needed several bins, since I had to clear a lot of weeds which would be perfect for recycling as compost. Everywhere I went for the next two weeks, I saw pallets in dumpsters, which their owners were only too pleased to let me have. In no time I had acquired enough pallets for six bins. I never see pallets now, not because they are not there but because I am not focused on them. The bins were painted as I acquired them with non toxic green waterproof preservative and transported straight to the site and erected and the compost building began.

right purpose

If we think of Zen as minimalism and clean lines, it may seem that filling your garden with junk is the complete opposite of what the subject is about. I have seen many organic gardens which look like junk heaps, but I have also seen many which are neat and tidy and which look identical to all the other gardens around them.

Recycling materials in a useful and productive way means we turn them into something which works for a purpose, they do not become the purpose themselves. I have seen pallets used as decking. If they had just been set down as they were, they would have looked very tacky, but additional slats were put in and they were stained and indistinguishable from their retail counterparts which would have cost a fortune.

"Seeking the Mind
within the mind,
is not this the
greatest of all
mistakes?"

Seng-T'san

Human Nature

Foresight

Blandness

Agreeableness

Youthfulness

Intuition

Comparison

Criticism

Reasoning

Causality

Planning

Humor

Mirthfulness

Wit

Comparison

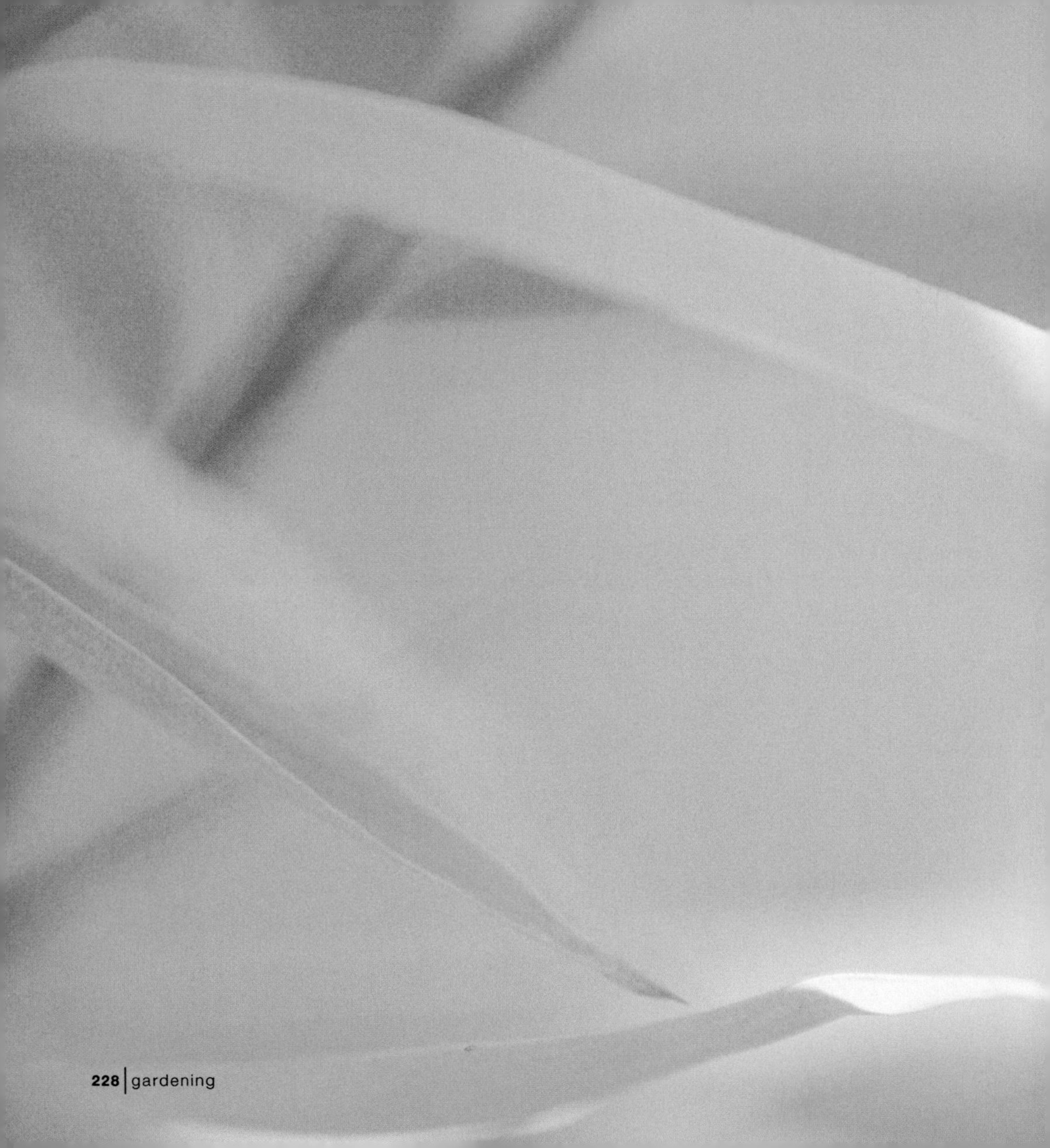

lawns

"Is mowing the lawn Zen?" While raking white gravel may be considered to be more Zen than mowing the lawn, lawn mowing can be relaxing and therapeutic, and can be as Zen or as not Zen as any other gardening task, depending on your purpose in doing it and the perceived outcome. Obsession, though, is altogether a different matter. Suzuki likens Zen practice to a railway track. You appreciate the signs you see along the way, but you do not become hooked into the track itself. He suggests that sometimes when young people travel around the world to find themselves, what they achieve in sitting and concentrating and bring back with them is more of a show than a lifestyle. It is the same as raking a gravel garden simply because you consider it Zen.

alternatives

It is easy to forget that grass is a plant and that it has similar needs to other plants. It appears at both ends of the care spectrum—as the most tended and the most neglected. Like other plants, it has to be in the right place to thrive. Too wet, and the moss takes over. Too dry, and the clover does. Plants grow where they are happy. If a lawn dies in a dry position and the clover thrives, why not have a clover lawn? And why apply moss killer to grass in which the only green part is the moss itself? Japanese gardeners love moss. It serves them as grass does us and suits the climate and damp areas where it is used.

There is nothing better to remind you of the mountains than a moss covered rock, with a maple leaf carefully placed for contrast to remind you of the forests. Chamomile is another substitute and needs cutting only twice a year, but I have never really seen one that works when it is walked on a lot. In out of the way places as a feature it is fine, but football and chamomile do not go well together. I like "Mind Your Own Business," Soleirolia soleirolii, but then I have never had a garden damp enough to grow it and I am told it can be a menace. But I like the ageless look of it, like the moss gardens in Japanese temples.

spiking lawns

There is so much snobbishness about lawns, particularly in the spiking of them in the fall. Preferring to let the worms do the work, I do not indulge in this ritual, but I can see it could become a Zen practice. The traditional way is to rake all the moss, fallen leaves, and other debris up in the fall and to walk up and down the lawn with the garden fork, sinking the prongs into the ground every six inches or so. Then finely sieved compost and a lawn tonic are spread around and brushed into the lawn. In the absence of rain, the lawn is watered and put to rest for the winter. There is now a tool for every task, and it is possible to purchase spiked rollers and spiked shoes to do the job more quickly. The latter sends the gardening elite and those aspiring to it into a frenzy of bad tastism. In his tongue in cheek *Yew and non-Yew: Gardening for Horticultural Climbers*, John Bartholomew tells of the sad plight of one wearing such shoes who became stuck in the lawn, causing much merriment in the neighborhood.

Wisdom is sometimes nearer where we stoop

Than when we soar…   William Wordsworth

bindweed

There are two virtues in life which should be valued above all other—humility and humor. The ability to achieve humility and to admit that you are wrong, or do not know, and the ability to laugh at yourself and life are characteristics to develop and treasure. There is one aspect of gardening which calls both for humility and humor, and that is confronting bindweed—something altogether more successful and resourceful than you and which can cause a lifetime of frustration and anger.

If you have bindweed, you will know only too well that whatever you do, it wins every time. It is possible to keep it within reasonable limits by spraying with a powerful chemical. However, bindweed conveniently coils around every other plant in the bed both above and below ground, ensuring that, if we spray, we will finish off every other plant too. Using chemicals is not an option for those who prefer to use organic methods, particularly near food crops.

Over the years I turned to learned tomes to find the answer and questioned "experts" closely. All I found was a wall of silence. Books rarely mention it, largely I think, since it is not good publishing policy to write about something with no solution.

Those with reputations to uphold, too, give an impression that we are worrying unduly and that time and patience will overcome this minor difficulty as they move on hastily to the next question. I have made all the classic bindweed mistakes. I have dug a border which had a tiny amount in one spot and raked the soil around until I had distributed it far and wide. I have made the mistake of assuming that, since I had back breakingly double-dug an asparagus bed, that I would be free of it, only to discover that the asparagus made wonderful supports for the bindweed. I have mulched with a four inch layer of straw and, while this brings many of the bindweed's spaghetti-like roots to the surface so that you can peel them off like a rug, they are still attached to a root a mile deep into the soil, which sends up even more stems the following year!

I have had ample opportunity to study the habits of bindweed, and because the older I get, the more I need to kneel or sit, I am actually working much closer to the ground. When you get to where the action is, you begin to see things differently. We have been concentrating on the wrong thing. The spaghetti-like roots are what have been keeping us preoccupied, but the real problem may be quite different. By getting really close to the soil, you will see thousands of miniscule white filaments around the thick roots. I suspect these are the real reason for the weed's success. I have no solution, except that I become even more convinced that the no dig policy is right. Let sleeping weeds lie.

instinct

It is a fact that a gardener is just as likely to be able to predict the weather as a TV weather presenter, as the former works on the likelihood based on experience of weather patterns, the feel of the air, and the behavior of animals, while the latter works on measurement. What measurements cannot take into consideration is the unpredictable changes which occur in the natural world, the sudden change in wind direction, the effect of a volcano exploding on the far side of the world, and so on. When our predecessors lived on the land and worked closely with the natural forces, they became attuned to any phenomena which would give them clues which could enable them to grow their crops effectively.

In a similar way, by concentrating on what is going on around you will be able to attune yourself more finely into the world of your garden. Why analyze why you always have aphids on your petunias when all you have to do is attend to their life cycle and plant at a different time, to encourage them to find other places to live. Concentration is a heightening of the senses enabling us to respond to the world around us in an appropriate way. We have no need to waste our energy and time on analysis or agonising, but on being aware and accepting of what is happening and acting appropriately.

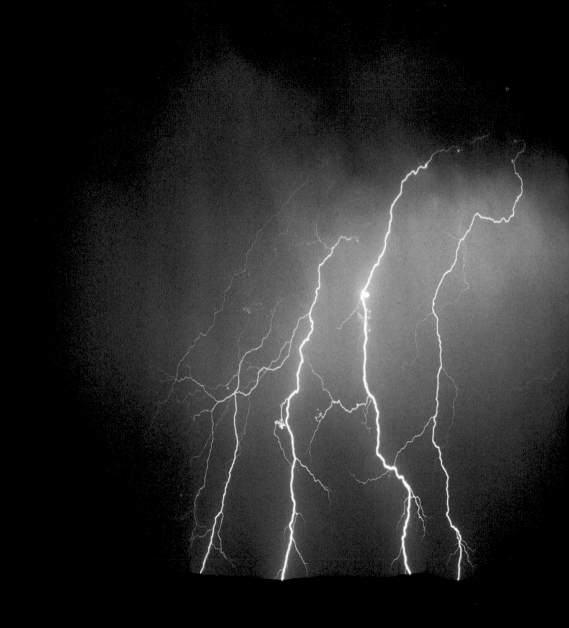

"you wish to see;

listen.

hearing is a step toward

vision."

"Painters
manipulate color
the way birds
know bugs and
squirrels nuts,
and how to codify
the instinct or
teach it is
daunting."

Robert Dash

senses

Our gardens speak to us through our senses. We usually concentrate on what we can see, but the others also come into play, along with that other sixth sense, or intuition. Everyone perceives the world in a different way. Go into any two gardens and you will be able to tell which are the favorite colors of the gardener, and from that you will usually be able to tell something of the personality of the owner. This is an observation rather than a rule, but many women prefer the more tranquil colors—the dark blues, the pinks, and the white, which are yin colors, while males often prefer the fiery reds and oranges, which are yang. The world is changing and women are becoming more yang and men more yin. It will be interesting to observe how this affects future garden design.

garden design

with the

five

elements

What we choose to
have in our gardens can be affected by how we feel
and can affect how we respond emotionally and psychologically.
While not a design tool to be followed absolutely, the five elements into which
those in the East have classified everything in the universe can offer us clues as to
why different shapes and colors affect us in certain ways. Take the metal element. The
quality of metal is heavy and solid. It is represented by round and oval shapes. In the
garden, hefty trees like the coniferous Thuja have a metal quality. When I see such trees on
either side of an entrance I am always reminded of nightclub bouncers—solid and
menacing. This is the yang form of metal. The yin form has an altogether different feel.
Standard box or bay balls or ivy balls on poles are lighter, nod their heads like
clowns and make you feel jolly. All white gardens have the quality of
metal: still and cold, overwhelming in a large space,
but cooling in a hot conservatory.

working philosophy

"In Zen
the important
thing is to stop
the course of
the mind."
Zen saying

I have spent a large part of my life daydreaming, imagining how the garden would be if it was twice the length, if I had room for a craved-for Cornus alternifolia, and if I had the resources to build the conservatory of my dreams. The fact is that these are merely dreams and what a lot of time is wasted dreaming about what might have been or what might be—if only. With the right sort of concentration we can achieve what is realistic in the here and now. Zen is a working philosophy because it enables us to get where we want to be in the course of our everyday lives. Mohammed suggested that, "Contemplation for an hour is better than formal worship for sixty years," but this implies taking time out from the regular routine in order to try to do something different. Zen goes further, enabling us to still the mind and experience what is important through whatever we are doing at the time.

The Biodynamic method of weed control involves treating like with like as in homeopathic medicine. There are two methods of treating persistent weeds, such as bindweed, and in the absence of more traditional solutions it is worth a try. I have known it to work superbly on Japanese knotweed, one of the most troublesome weeds around.

eradicating weeds

The Ash Method
Method 1
Gather seeds of the weeds you wish to eradicate and place them in a paper or cardboard container on a woodburning or charcoal stove. Burn at a very high temperature, until a gray ash is formed. When the ash is cool it can be sprinkled on the area which you wish to clear, but you will obviously have only enough ash for a small area.

Method 2

To make the ash go further, you can make a homeopathic solution which can then be used as a spray.

- Place a good pinch of the ash in a small jar and shake for 3 minutes
- Add this to 1/2 cup of water and shake for 3 minutes
- Add to 4 cups of water and shake for 3 minutes
- Add to 2 gallons of water and stir for 3 minutes
- Take 1 teaspoon of this solution and add 2 teaspoons of water and shake for 3 minutes
- Add to 1/2 cup of water and shake for 3 minutes
- Add to 4 cups of water and shake for 3 minutes
- Add to 2 gallons of water and stir for 3 minutes
- Spray at the rate of 2 1/4 cups to 120 square yards three times, with three hours between each spray

The Root Method

Place roots and stems of plants like bindweed, couch, and Japanese knotweed in a barrel and cover it. Leave until rotted down, stirring occasionally. When they are quite broken down, sieve the liquid and spray every day for three days in the evening.

chapter 7

right attention: quality

Meditation: "The Tao's principle is spontaneity." Lao Tzu

The best experiences are those not planned—an incredible sunset, the sighting of a rare bird, the happening on an incredible view over a bay or a landscape. Despite our ordered, regulated lives there is still much to wonder at. The Diamond Sutra says "The past is ungraspable, the present is ungraspable, the future is ungraspable." This being so, we have to live every moment of our lives to the full in order not to waste one precious moment. If we rush out to look at rainbows, catch snow, and crunch on leaves in the fall, we retain a childlike and receptive mind, needing no ulterior motives and no conclusions.

priorities

To work in a Zen way is to work giving your whole attention to the task in hand, without being sidetracked by the 101 other jobs which are waiting to be done. I never fail to be impressed when I travel to France at the morning sweeping ritual. At about 9AM, the noise of brooms brushing the pavements outside homes and shops is impressive. It is a ritual which takes little time but creates a tidy start to the day, much as cleaning and putting away garden tools at the end of it does. How much nicer it is to begin the following day knowing where everything is and knowing that you will not have to unravel the grass from the mower before you can use it. Right attention given at the right time means that life runs smoothly.

"the more you look, the less you observe."

Thoreau

observation

When we pay particular attention to something, we lose the wider picture. If you are working in the garden and your robin is alongside as you go about your business, he will go about his. If you stand and watch him, he will become conscious of the fact and will not be able to act naturally, because what he is actually waiting for is for you to dig his dinner and not at all interested in observing you. Be part of your environment and not apart from it.

cherry blossom

In Japan they have a special word for "flower watching," particularly watching cherry blossom. So important is the event as a spring marker, that some firms arrange staff outings to visit parks when the blossom is at its best. I traveled to Washington in April last year and got a regular update from my host on the state of the blossom before I arrived. TV and radio broadcasts keep everyone up to date and bets are taken on the exact day it will come into bloom. It was early last year and I missed it by a week. The mass of cherry blossom is an indication of spring and the blossom billows like a ballerina's dress for a week or two—and then what? What about summer and autumn and winter? In the Zen garden, we mark these seasons too. A single blossom is as powerful a marker as a mass of it. The single flower on my clematis in August is, in fact, a more powerful image than the mass that cascades over the garden wall in spring.

the
gate
post

Helen and John Philbrick, at the forefront of the
Biodynamic movement in the United States, told this
story of a visit to their garden in Missouri by Dr Pfeiffer, a
leading Biodynamic author and researcher. The peach tree by
their gate had once been home to a borer, long since departed.
Nevertheless, they could not cure the tree of the infection in the
trunk. Dr Pfeiffer's advice was to mend the fence post, a response
rather reminiscent of those proffered by the Zen masters from the Rinsai
school. The shelf fungi on the fence post, seeing the post as a dead tree,
were working away at a worn part in order to do their job of breaking down rotting
wood and the spores were also attracted to the wound on the tree. If the post was
fixed, there would be no more spores around to attack the tree, illustrating that we need
to develop powers of observation and deduction in the garden.

"Observe all kinds
of coincidences —
as what kinds of
birds come with
what flowers…"
Thoreau

coincidence

There is no doubt that if we all kept gardening diaries, we
would see patterns in the behavior of plants and wildlife in
the garden and in their interaction. Very little that happens in
the garden happens by chance, and few things could be
termed coincidence. Things happen for a very good reason.
We do not always need to know what the reason is, but just
to observe the patterns will help. Take flying ants. Who
would be wanting to host a lunch party on flying ant day, any
more than you would want to be hanging your best white
damask table linen on the line when the starlings pay their
annual visit to the elderberry tree. If we watch, we can read
the signs and predict their coming. Alternatively, we can
keep a note in a diary one year and be amazed at their time-
keeping during the next.

weeds

It is no coincidence that weeds grow where they do, and they can tell us so much about an environment.

Weeds are an indication of soil conditions; if it is too acid, often an indication of lack of air, we will see horsetail and dock.

Legumes can indicate a poor sandy soil and plantains, chickweed, and dandelions are usually to be found where we frequently walk on soil and compact it.

If nettles move in, let them do their work in healing a sick soil and you will be rewarded by a fertile loam.

pests

It is no coincidence either that pests arrive when and where they do. There is a pest for everything—a gooseberry saw-fly, an asparagus beetle, and other specialists. Why then do we encourage them? Why do we plant all our asparagus together and all our gooseberries together. It is like putting up an enormous restaurant sign. In forest gardens and potagers, planting is mixed, so that the plants and wildlife tend to regulate each other. It is very rare to see infestations of any particular insect in the wild. By planting more naturally, and being aware of the life cycles of the insects we wish to discourage, we can avoid planting in places and at times when we are providing the perfect conditions for pests to flourish.

"Having examined the appearance of the thing one seizes upon its essence."

Ching Hao

the essence

When I was a child I used to watch clouds. No two were ever the same and as we drove along, they would change shape and make images in the sky. Sometimes they would look like a face, other times like an animal, and I would give them names. I liked the big puffy clouds best and I learned that the name cumulus covered all of them. I learned about weather systems and the effect of the wind on the clouds, about air pressure, and so on, but it was never as interesting as giving them individual names. I liked to look at stones too, fascinated by the intricate markings on them and at trees, wondering how there could be so many combinations of the same pattern on the trunks.

In ancient China, everything was considered to have an energy or life force and names, often of animals, were used to describe them. Mountains were allotted specific names—for example, Young Dragon Watching its Mother. The information about the shape of mountains and their relationship to those living close by was crucial. The weather dragons in the sky cry their tears onto the mountains. The tears become the blood in mountain dragons' veins and are channeled onto the plains below to irrigate the fields. It becomes quite crucial then what type of clouds sit above the mountains, how much rain they cry, and how it falls onto the land below, because if the house is not in the right place, it will be flooded out in the rainy season. If the water is channeled away from the fields, then the crops will suffer.

By observing regional weather patterns and the space that our garden occupies, we can position our seating areas using them as protection from the wind, be aware of the swirling currents set up near the corners and in some courtyard spaces created by a building's irregular shape and we can create water flows which create a healthy haven for wildlife and plants.

the golden carp

In China, the carp is regarded as a symbol for ambition, achievement, and success. Legend has it that every year in the third month the carp swim up the Yellow River to the Dragon Gate. The currents are fierce and against them, and only the sturdiest make it. The final test is at the end, where the waters gush down from the mountain and only a very few will be able to make the last final leap up the waterfall to the calm waters beyond. Those who do make it are turned into dragons, the symbol of the Emperor. One evening, earlier this century, Victor Schauberger, an Austrian naturalist, sat by a stream waiting to catch a trout poacher. As he watched in the moonlight, a group of trout suddenly dispersed as a particularly large fish swam up from beneath them, twisting and dancing in the current. Suddenly it began to swim up the waterfall and then disappeared. Schauberger did not have an exact scientific theory to which he could attach the phenomenon, but knew, from his studies of the way water moves, that "it was a case of a synchronicity of events, leading to a unique form of movement." Movement which overcomes the force of gravity and enables fish of a certain weight and shape to rise upwards, in much the same way that wind spirals can lift frogs, fish, and even houses into the air and move them along. We tend to search for meaning and explanations, and in doing so are apt to dismiss phenomena for which an explanation cannot be found. There are many things about the way the natural world works that we do not know and many for which science may never find the answers. The Zen way is to pay attention to what we see and go with the flow without analyzing the reasons why.

awarenes

"An ancient pond;
A frog leaps in;
The sound of water."

Basho

So many images,

so many associations,

all from seventeen syllables.

Such is the quality of

Zen attention.

water features

It has become fashionable to introduce water features into gardens and the range is vast, from magnificent carved stone fountains to a tiny trickle over pebbles. Each feature has its own sound and it is worth sitting by them for a while before you buy, to see how it affects you. One of the nicest I have ever seen was in a garden in Dorset. The fountain stood in the middle of the pond, its three jets rising six feet or so into the air and falling in a glistening sprinkle much as the stars fall from firework rockets. On a plinth nearby stood the three graces, huddled together as if chattering in an animated way and a pot of giant alliums stood alongside, their round purple heads bobbing in the breeze. The whole effect was busy and animated, a perfect spot for a coffee morning with friends.

prunin

The simplest solution to finding the correct time to prune each plant is to pay attention to its growth patterns. Pruning at the wrong time of year will mean losing the flower buds, and it puts the plant out of rhythm.

- When growing a tree or shrub for its flowers, prune after flowering but before the plant puts all it energy into seed production at the expense of next year's buds.

- When a plant has fruited, prune back to a shoot which will develop flower buds next year.

- Stems which flower and fruit in the same season are usually cut out after fruiting.

- Those which make growth one year and flower and fruit the next are trimmed back to a flowering bud in the fall of the first year.

Simple, but how we agonize and how many mistakes we make! The more we prune, the more vigorously the plant will grow next year. Gardeners in the East have got pruning down to a fine art, knowing the best ways to make the trees grow to their full advantage and to reflect their individual characteristics.

time

Looking to the needs of plants and selecting the right places for them to be in terms of soil, aspect, and their neighbors enables us to provide for them the best we can. Performing the various garden tasks as and when they are required will ensure that things run smoothly. Timing is as important as placement. Planting with the natural rhythms of the universe will enable our plants to thrive.

The earth is a living, breathing organism and is as receptive to the gravitational pull of the moon as the seas whose tides it controls. The earth breathes out in the morning and in the afternoon it breathes in, as the moon's gravity affects the different sides of the globe. At night it rests. The expansive breathing out time in the morning is the best for planting out leaf crops and the breathing in time in the afternoon for sowing seeds and root crops which need to get a firm foothold in the soil. In addition, the monthly cycle of the moon, and its path through the different constellations, indicates the best days and times of the month for planting different types of plants according to the qualities we are searching for—the leaf, root, fruit, seed, or flower.

be born and a time to die, a time to plant, and a time to pluck up what is planted...

Ecclesiates 3, 1-2

when to plant

When I acquired my first garden, I was a complete novice. We bought a house during a property boom and we knew we had to move quickly. We bought the house in the dark—literally. What my eyes could not see, my nose told me was the place. The garden was huge when I finally saw it and I needed help. Our neighbor was a treasure, and often a hand would often appear over the fence with a tray of something tempting to plant. From the garden on the other side would come a warning—"Don't you plant those until Thursday," followed by an accompanying rumble of incredulity from the donor's side. But I listened—and it worked. The little old man who leaned on the gate sky watching every night started me on the path I was to follow and it seemed right.

If you continue
this simple practice every day,
you will obtain some wonderful power.
Before you attain it, it is something wonderful,
but after you attain it, it is nothing special.

Sazuki

Planting information based on the moon cycle, and occasionally on the sun cycle, is still given in almanacs published all over the world—the *T'ung Shu*, sold in Chinese communities everywhere and the *Farmer's Almanac* widely available in the United States among them. There is also much written by the Roman writers on the subject. Cato (234–149 BCE) in his treatise on agriculture gave useful advice, such as, "The trimming of the olive trees should begin fifteen days before the vernal equinox; you can trim to advantage from this time for forty-five days." This advice will have taken into account the growth pattern of the olive, the temperature and likely weather conditions, the cycles of fungal diseases, and soil conditions.

Depending on the type of plant and their growth patterns, plants thrive best when planted at the correct time in the monthly lunar cycle. Those who plant by the moon perceive the different qualities of each part of the plant as being governed by an element and the elements are governed by the movement of the moon through each of the twelve star constellations every month. Planting is usually postponed for a day or two on either side of a new and a full moon, and near eclipses. Each lunar month is approximately twenty-nine days long and is divided into four quarters.

planting by the moon

1st Quarter		
Plant and harvest leaf plants	in the Water constellations	Cancer Scorpio Pisces
Plant flowers which produce seed outside the plant	in the Air constellation	Libra
Harvest fruit and seed	in the Fire constellations	Aries Leo Sagittarius
Harvest flowers	in the Air constellations	Gemini Aquarius
2nd Quarter		
Plant leaf plants which produce seed within the plant	in the Water constellations	Cancer Scorpio Pisces
Plant flowers which produce seed inside the plant	in the Air constellation	Libra
Harvest as in the 1st Quarter		
3rd Quarter		
Plant root crops, bulbs, tubers Harvest root crops	in the Earth constellations	Taurus Capricorn
Plant perennial, trees, and shrubs for foliage	in the Water constellations	Pisces Cancer Scorpio
Transplant and take cuttings		
Plant perennials, trees, and shrubs for flowers	In the Air constellation	Libra
4th Quarter		

A barren time. Use for routine maintenance, mowing, and pruning.

chapter 8

right understanding: spirituality

"The servant of the Tao,

realizing the perfect beauty of the universe, attains understanding." Lao Tzu

For most of us, words are a barrier to the expression of the soul. Gardens have become the outlet for spirituality which cannot be spoken with words. When we create a garden, we have the raw ingredients readily available to create a masterpiece. As the Chinese cataloged mountain and river formations, so the Japanese cataloged how to set stones and rocks in the correct manner to present their right faces to the world. In doing so, they preserved their heritage and knowledge. In order to use the information, however, it requires an understanding of the meaning behind the diagrams, since something more than words is crucial to grasping the true nature of the mountains and water, how they sit and flow, and work together.

an unspoken

We are told that it is impossible to express Zen in words. In 1968, D.T. Suzuki wrote "The contradiction so puzzling to the ordinary way of thinking comes from the fact that we have to use language to communicate our inner experience which by its very nature transcends linguistics."

Z language

Five years before he wrote this, W. Heisenberg was writing something very similar. "The problem of language here is really serious. We wish to speak in some way about the structure of atoms... but we cannot speak about atoms in everyday language." Quantum physics and Zen are closely linked by an inability to express the meaning of life in words. One group will strive to do so and the other will just accept what is.

connecting

Many people are now removed from the natural world. This has been a process spanning four centuries. Written in England in 1782, *The Torrington Diaries* express the following insight:

"Enclosure of the common land was a bad job and minded all us poor folk. Before it, we had our garden, our bees, our share of a flock of sheep, and the feeding of our geese. And could cut turf for fuel."

After the enclosure of land by wealthy landowners, the poor migrated to towns in search of work and suffered hardship. Enclosure began in Tudor times in the sixteenth century and has continued to the present time. When people do not have access to the natural world they display the same characteristics as caged animals. They become disturbed. Architects and governments have realized that high rise solutions are not the answer to growing populations, and are increasingly designing low-level housing in green environments. Meanwhile, community gardens provide for those who actively pursue a connection with the earth.

change

Quantum physicists have discovered that since nothing is static and everything is constantly changing, it is not possible to quantify exactly the structure and behavior of the universe. There is no language to express it. Yet Zen can help by offering a concept, that of yin and yang, which can be described as a positive and negative force, pulling against each other to produce a reaction. Each has a tiny seed of the other which acts as the catalyst for change. It is this theory of change which has moved quantum physics on from conventional science—in which everything can be classified and remains static—towards a more Zen view of how things work.

Plants, aided by the wind and by insects and birds, swap pollen with others in the same species and produce a different plant. Human beings have taken a hand in making sure that we retain the characteristics of say, white petunias, or a certain variety of cabbage, by controlling the pollination process. But whatever plant is produced, it is a unique individual, capable—if left to its own devices—of cross pollinating with a red petunia or another variety of cabbage, to produce something quite different from either parent plant.

$$3y - 2 = z$$

a theory of

John Barrow, writing in 1991, suggested that scientists are still searching for the "Theory of Everything," much as our ancestors were. Every world religion and each nation's mythology indicate that they thought they had found the answers. When scientists come up with their ultimate theory, it can only be based on mathematical calculation and logic, and will be set in stone, but will be based on the information which they have available at the time. The holistic Buddhist method allows for the fact that things evolve and change and what is fact to us now will be history tomorrow. Barrow suggests that it is not that the ancient Eastern viewpoint is wrong, "just premature" for modern Western thinking. In the West, nature is perceived as many component parts which, according to Francis Bacon, should be "extracted" and nature "tortured" to give up her secrets.

Ever since the sixteenth century, he and others like him took a mathematical view of nature. Intuition, feeling, and senses were discounted as being merely reactions and of little worth. Later, Newton, whose theories still reign supreme in much of scientific thinking, demanded proof for every phenomena in the natural world. There were challengers. In Germany, Goethe and Rudolf Steiner, founder of the Biodynamic farming and gardening movement, suggested that there was a spiritual side to science, and felt we should look at natural phenomena, rather than behind them, and should observe the signs they give to us.

$$5y = z$$

everything

The Eastern view of nature, expressed by Chu Hsi in 1200 is similar. Li, or nature, is made up of "the innumerable vein like patterns included in the Tao"—the way of the world. Yet we will not even mention the miniscule vein-like filaments of bindweed in books, because it makes untidy the view that we can overcome all things and the way in which we wish to perceive the art of gardening. Scientist Thoreau suggests "If you want to be wise, learn science and then forget it." While science has produced some very worthy ideas, it is a pity that these cannot always be harnessed in such a way as to benefit and not manipulate the natural world.

conservation

A significant gesture we can make to our successors is to leave them the world as we found it so that they too can experience the diversity of species in the plant and animal worlds and can inherit a world which will support them and keep them and their descendants healthy for generations to come. Fortunately, we are reaching the point where we appreciate that it is better to see a butterfly fluttering around the garden than pinned out in a drawer, and to see elephants roaming free in their natural environment rather than imprisoned in a concrete enclosure. We are already seeing a move away from the indiscriminate use of chemicals in gardens and in the countryside. Each one of us can play a part in ensuring our heritage if we keep focused on the fact that what we do now will affect not only this generation, but those to come.

the valley

On a recent trip to the United States, I was invited to the home of a family who owned a large valley. From their house they had a wide ranging view to the fields beyond the woodland which bordered their land. The woods surrounded the house on all sides, save for an opening across to the hills in front of the sitting room window. It was on this hill that developers were building new houses. As we sat, a family of deer crossed the opening. Several minutes later, a yellow bulldozer followed the same path, the significance clear to everyone in the room. The family were united in wishing to preserve their heritage for future generations of the family, angry at the threat to their view, and dismayed at the thought of being overlooked as they swam in their pool. How they were to go about dealing with it was in dispute. One half of the family wanted to plant fast growing conifers to obliterate the sight of the new houses as quickly as possible. The other could see ahead to the inconsistency of a wall of conifers in the middle of an ancient deciduous wood which would, in time, become a scar on the landscape. By planting in keeping with the landscape, they may never see the result of their actions, but will preserve the landscape for the future. In the short term, a few well placed shrubs closer to the house will draw their view and those of their new neighbors away from the sights that they do not want either party to see.

courage

You must be in charge of the

change you wish to see in the world.

The Zen way is to follow our own path and to take personal responsibility for the natural world in a personal way. It is easy to become angry and to argue, but ultimately we are only responsible for our own thoughts and actions. The best way to offer our views on what works is by actually working hard to put them into practice. The path may not be easy and there will be problems on the way, but these can be overcome if we are true to what we believe in and follow our consciences. The path we follow can be expressed in the way we plan and undertake our gardening activities. The various elements in the garden can act as a reminder of that path and can illustrate for us the journey ahead.

the journey

The journey through a garden can represent the journey through life. This can best be seen in the tea gardens, where every element has a symbolic meaning for those who come there. While we cannot adopt the symbols of another culture into our own in a meaningful way, we can appreciate how they represent archetypal notions which represent the journey and we can use them in a personal way within the spirit of our own environment.

"Japanese gardens ask that you go beyond the garden spiritually. That you look at the garden, not merely as an object but also as a path into the realms of the spirit."

Makoto Ooka

the gate

The garden gate marks a transition between the outer and inner world; our neighborhood and our inner space; our outer persona and our inner selves. The gate moves us through from one set of circumstances to another, luring us on to begin a new journey, and brings with it the suggestion of transformation.

Approach	The approach to the gate is symbolic in itself. The direct approach can suggest that we are ready and prepared to begin the journey, or if we approach from the side we may tarry a while to take in the surroundings before making the leap. Traditionally, when approaching an Indian temple, a clockwise circuit is made around the gate before entering, to shake off worldly matters before entering the inner sanctum.
View	The gate leads into the enclosed space of our inner sanctum, and the enclosure acts as the backdrop to the garden—the frame to the painting. The gate and all the smaller gates and windows within the garden mark transition points and entries to new spaces, while in themselves representing the important concept of "nothingness." The view is not symmetrical, resembling the natural world, and nothing acts as a central focal point.
Pillars	The pillars on either side of the gate suggest a balance between male and female, fear and hope, goodness and evil—the balance of yin and yang.
Crossbeam	The crossbeam links the two and as we bow to pass under it, we demonstrate humility as we approach the transforming process ahead.
Door	The door in the gate can welcome or intimidate, hiding the journey from us.
Lock and Key	Represents a barrier, an indication of the fears and prejudices which prevent us from embarking on the journey and the key—as it pierces the center of the lock—awakens our consciousness and shows us the way ahead.
Threshold	Crossing the threshold signifies taking the plunge and embarking on our journey down an unknown path.

the path

The path symbolizes our psychological journey through life, designed to awaken our conscience and enable us to gain wisdom on the way. There will be obstructions, twists and turns to confuse us, and we will encounter disappointments and snags on the way. If we keep to the path and journey with the right attitudes and emotions we will ultimately achieve our journey's end.

Straight Path   A straight path can denote confidence and focus, but may encourage us to move too quickly without giving due consideration to things we might meet on the way.

Winding Path   The winding path will carry us forward and allow us to consider all things before we reach the journey's end.

Spiral Path   The spiral path can lead us to an inwardly focused point where we can concentrate our minds on where we are heading.

Radial Path   Paths which radiate from a central point indicate that our conscious thoughts are moving on to a higher plane and that we are moving on.

Crossing Paths   Crossing paths indicate a place where change occurs, a change of focus or direction or a chance meeting which will change our lives. Too many crossing paths illustrate that we are not focused and cannot still the mind. Those where the connections flow together lead us onward to new realms of thought.

> "It is not the road you walk, it is in the walking."
>
> Vatsyayana

Materials

Our journey can be speeded up or slowed down according to the materials used. If we walk along a run of regular paving slabs, and are suddenly confronted with a patch of cobble stones, we have to slow down and be mindful of our footing, as we do when the stones are uneven. The scrunch of gravel concentrates our every step and keeps us focused and aware. Walking on bark will add a spring to our step.

Direction

The laying of stones and paving can direct our journey through the garden. Laid longways they can stretch our vision onwards, but with the shorter side facing, our journey is slowed. Stepping stones can draw our passage left and right with stopping places indicated merely by laying several stones together.

Stairs and Slopes

Stairs and slopes allow us to contemplate the relationship between heaven as we rise and earth as we fall enabling us to see the ultimate goal and realize that it can be achieved here on earth. As we rise, we have clarity and have hope that our dreams can be realized. As we fall, doubts and fears can hinder our progress.

Bridges

Bridges offer us a depth and spread of vision. Having reached a lake or river, which we might perceive as an insurmountable barrier, we can see a way forward. In the *I Ching*, the Chinese oracle and book of wisdom, crossing the water means taking the plunge and moving towards what you hope to achieve.

the seat

The seat marks the point when we reach our ultimate goal. It marks the resting place at the culmination of our journey. Here we find illumination and self knowledge and experience rebirth into a higher level of consciousness.

freedom

You can begin the journey now—this minute. If you decide to wait until you have been on vacation, or finished the latest project, then you are not yet ready to begin. Similarly, when you sit down and struggle to understand, you will never do so because you will only be drawing on your own resources, limited by where you are now. If you read many books and look for meaning in the words of others, you may be guided and they may give credence to your current points of view, but they cannot help you to understand. Ever since I was first married, I have written down words of wisdom which have meant something to me at the time. Leafing through the book recently, I realized that what I had in front of me was a record of my life—hopes, dreams, desires, relationships, and understanding. What seemed important even last year has long since become something I do not concern myself with now. There is no need for the book, just as there is no need to cling to any of the possessions, relationships, and thoughts which clog up our lives and prevent us from moving on.

When we can detach from possessions, we are free to express ourselves in our own way; it is at this point that we create something special.

"It is preoccupation with possessions, more than anything else, that prevents us from living freely and nobly."

Bertrand Russell

enlightenment

Having written this book does not mean that I am enlightened, merely that I am aware of the path. As Lao Tzu suggested that "Those who know do not speak and those who speak do not know." If you are reading it, you may not be aware of the path or may be on it and looking for clues to help you on your way. If you are enlightened you will not be reading it anyway, since in the words of an ancient Hindu saying, "When people reach the highest perfection, it is nothing special; it is their normal condition."

Zen Saying

Before enlightenment
I chopped wood and carried water;
after enlightenment,
I chopped wood and carried water.

nature as the mighty whole

The Zen way is to come to understanding through whatever you are doing now. Hakuin suggests that "Not knowing how near the truth is, people seek it far away, what a pity! They are like him who, in the midst of water, cries thirst so imploringly." What we seek is all around us and is expressed in the natural world. For most of us, we come close to nature in the garden and can find what we are seeking there.

"...one interior life
In which all beings live with God, themselves
Are God, existing in the mighty whole,
Indistinguishable as the cloudless east
Is from the cloudless west, when all
The hemisphere is one cerulean blue."

Wordsworth

seed saving

One sure way of preserving a favorite plant or vegetable is to save your own seed. The great botanic gardens are in the process of collecting seed from every plant in the world to protect plant species for posterity. Other schemes also collect and preserve seeds of popular plants which have been removed from commercial lists and this approach encourages individuals to collect seed and make the seed available to others.

Ground Rules for Seed Saving

- Only save seeds from plants which have been grown organically and have not been genetically modified
- Save seeds from plants which have cropped well and flourished in normal soil and weather conditions for the locality
- Keep crops of the same family apart to prevent cross pollination. Half a mile is a good safety net
- Do not save the seed of plants which have bolted
- Do not save seed from hybrid plants. It will not germinate the following year

Storage

Seed must be kept in dry, cool conditions. A sachet of silica gel, available in photographers' shops, can be useful for keeping moisture out. Seeds will keep for the following number of years:

1 Onions, Parsnips
2 Peppers
3 Asparagus, Beans, Carrots, Lettuce, Peas
4 Squash, Tomatoes
5 Aubergines

"So that for all things out of a garden,
either of salads or fruits,
a poor man will eat better,
than he has one of his own,
than a rich man that has none.
And this is all I think of,
necessary and useful,
to know upon this subject."

William Temple—On Gardening, 1685

Sourcebooks, Inc.
P.O. Box 4410, Naperville, Illinois 60567-4410

TEL: (630) 961-3900
FAX: (630) 961-2168

Printed and bound in Italy
MQ 10 9 8 7 6 5 4 3 2 1

ISBN: 1-57071-686-2